*The Art of Being a*

# PITA

By Author
## SHANAH BELL

*The Art of Being a*

# PITA

# The Art of Being a PITA

The opinions expressed by the author are not necessarily those of
Wisdom House Books, Inc.

Published by Wisdom House Books, Inc.
Chapel Hill, North Carolina 27514 USA
1.919.883.4669 | www.wisdomhousebooks.com

Wisdom House Books is committed to excellence in the publishing industry.

Book design copyright © 2019 by Wisdom House Books, Inc. All rights reserved.

Cover and Interior design by Ted Ruybal

Published in the United States of America

Paperback ISBN: 978-1-7336017-0-2
LCCN: 2019901520

BIO003000    BIOGRAPHY & AUTOBIOGRAPHY / Business
BUS109000    BUSINESS & ECONOMICS / Women in Business
SEL027000    SELF-HELP / Personal Growth / Success

First Edition
14 13 12 11 10 / 10 9 8 7 6 5 4 3 2 1

# Table of Contents

## Table of Contents

# Preface

When I was younger, the message I was given was the same as everyone else from my generation. Success meant that you got a good, stable job, with a large company, had vacation days and benefits. You would work for them until you retired and live a happy, fairly uncomplicated life. Well, not only is that not reality, but it wasn't what I *ever* wanted my life to look like. As somebody who has never done things the conventional way, and has been a "hard learner" (as my mother likes to say), I went the unconventional route.

What I wish I had been told, instead, was to find what my "why" was. What was it that drove me in life? When you realize what your purpose is for getting out of bed every morning, then you know what your why is. Once you figure out your why, it becomes easier to discern how to incorporate that drive into a career, of sorts. I have found that, when I'm doing things that drive me, I am much more motivated to not only do a great job but to go above and beyond.

My why has always been to help people live their most accomplished and best life. I like to do this through food, primarily, but it has taken many different shapes throughout the years, depending on what people need from me. Basically, if the skills I have to offer can make their lives easier in any way, then I feel like I am doing what I am called to do. This is what drives me. After all, we all want the same things in life, just in different forms sometimes. We all want to be happy, be loved, be healthy, enjoy our lives, and feel like we are contributing something. Whatever form those things come in for you may differ from somebody else's, but the overarching message is the same.

So, what is your why? What unique perspective do you have on the world that you can incorporate into your skill set? When you figure this out, you will be much further ahead than most others. So, focus on what you bring to the table through your why, and you will not only go far in life but be a much happier person for it.

More often than not, creating a diverse skill set to pursue your why will only increase your level of happiness and satisfaction. This is because most of us are good at multiple things, not just one thing. Or to expand on this more, there are certain aspects to each job that we like more and are better at. So, utilizing the skills we develop that feel more in tune with our why increases our overall happiness, and in turn, our effectiveness in our careers.

When we feel like we are really using our skills to the best of our abilities to create positive change, in whatever form that comes in, we not only feel more appreciated but feel more satisfaction in our lives, as well. This is where diversity comes into play. When we diversify what we're doing to play to our larger strengths, we only increase the potential level of overall satisfaction exponentially. So why on Earth wouldn't we actively pursue this?

On top of this, learning new skills and increasing our diversity can only help increase our overall long-term cognition. There have been a few studies[1] done recently on how learning new skills affects things such as increasing the myelin sheath density (which increases the information flow in your brain), increasing problem solving skills; improving memory, and slowing age-related cognitive decline.

Increasing our diversity makes us better employees, better spouses, better friends, better problem solvers, and keeps our brains younger, longer. Therefore, learning new skills, and creating diversity, can only help us in the long-term game of life.

But on top of increasing your overall cognitive and problem-solving skills, incorporating more diversity into your work-life can drastically change how you look at work. When you aren't doing the same thing every single day, or working with the same people, there is an air of excitement that develops; there is less work drama, or none, because you aren't with the same people all the time. It's harder for the core work group to suck you into their misery if you aren't there all the time. Every day is almost like a vacation because you don't have to deal with the drama, and it's different than the day before.

I like to keep my schedule as diverse as possible because then I never get bored. I don't burn out from a job because I'm not doing the same thing every day. By working this way, I have trained my brain to shift tasks at a much faster rate than most other people. This not only makes my days more exciting, and my problem-solving skills pretty damn good, but makes me an excellent person to hire. I am faster, and more efficient, than a lot of other people I have worked with because I have developed this high level of diversity, which has, in turn, widened

---

1    https://www.health.harvard.edu/blog/learning-new-skill-can-slow-cognitive-aging-201604279502
     https://www.ncbi.nlm.nih.gov/pmc/articles/PMC4154531/
     https://onlinelibrary.wiley.com/doi/full/10.1002/ana.24158

my skill set beyond most "normal" levels. And it wasn't that hard to do.

I found things that interested me, that were in my wheelhouse at the time, and then began to expand on each skill. I pushed myself a little bit further outside of my comfort zone with each position on purpose. Because I knew that, if I could learn more about the position, or more skills within the position, I could make myself a more coveted employee. But on top of that, it would only increase what I could do for the rest of my life. So, by increasing my skills through diversifying, I was changing the rest of my life for the better, for as long as I shall live. Sounds like a pretty sweet deal, right?

I can't pinpoint the exact moment I realized what I was doing, as it has always seemed like second nature to me, but I do recall my high level of diversity when I was in high school and had multiple jobs. At the time, they were all in the food service industry, until the summer of my Junior year, but I did different things at each place, therefore, increasing my skill set right out of the gate. To make things more interesting, I went to two high schools my senior year (which I had to petition to do) and took college classes at night. This was during the '90s, when high school students didn't take college classes at night. Unlike today, when most high schools and colleges, in this area at least, offer dual enrollment. So, I was diversifying and increasing my myelin sheathing at a young age. It only stands to reason that I would keep it up throughout my life, and I have. I don't see it changing any time soon, either!

But as great as this sounds from a skill, problem-solving, and cognition perspective, this level of diversifying has had an effect on my personal life. My personal life has never been what the status quo is. Since I have always had my hands in so many different pots, and continue to push myself to learn new things every day, it stands to reason that my friend group is diverse. And it certainly is!

I have different friends for different things I like to do. It has been this way as long as I can remember. When I was younger, I tried to have a core group of friends (this was in high school, and we all know how tumultuous that can be!), but it never worked out well for me. No grass grows under my feet (another anecdote my mother has bestowed upon me!), so I keep moving and changing, fairly rapidly. Therefore, there have been a lot of friends that have come and gone in my life because I am no longer in a place where we have common ground.

Many, many years ago, this was a difficult thing for me to come to terms with. After all, another fallacy we are taught is that, as adults, we will have some childhood friends that really know us better than anybody else. That has not been the case for me. I have one childhood friend, Marianne, who I lived with in Ventura, CA and still speak to. But we live on opposite coasts and have completely different lives. We used to play street hockey and soccer together, and as adults, we both love hiking. Other than that, we don't have anything to talk about because we are in completely different places. There is nothing wrong with this, in my opinion, as I learned that everybody changes. And we don't all change along the same path. That doesn't make one of us good and the other bad, it just means that life has taken us in different directions, and I am okay with that.

So, I have friends I talk to about parenting, some I talk to about science, some I talk to about writing, some about food and nutrition, some about finances, some about hiking and camping, etc. You get the drift. But I don't spend time with all of them together in a group—I compartmentalize them. If I put all of my friends together in a room, they would, more than likely, have nothing to talk about, nor would they understand why I am friends with some of the other people in that room. They are just that diverse of a set of people, as I am just that diverse. But I love having different people to talk to about all of the different interests and skills I have. I just realize that we won't all see eye to eye on everything, and that is okay. As humans, we are never going to see eye to eye on everything. So keep that in mind.

With regard to my romantic relationships, my increased skill set and diversity has had an effect there, as well. Most of the men I have dated *loved* how diverse and how quick at problem-solving I was—In the beginning, at least. After that, they then began to hate it because it made them feel inferior. But in all reality, that is an insecurity thing on their part and really had nothing to do with me. I just made the wrong choices in partners. As I have gotten older, I've become wiser in my choice of romantic partners. Now, I have an awesome partner, Bryan, who not only loves my heightened problem-solving skills and diversity but supports me and pushes me to go further. I couldn't ask for a better partner because he is not afraid of who I am, but instead, uses me as inspiration to push himself further outside of his comfort zone. I got wiser, and pretty damn lucky, when I found him.

However, my increasing workload can have an effect on our relationship, especially as co-parents. We live in a blended family with five children, which can get a bit hairy sometimes. The weeks that I have more work on my plate, he does what he can to pick up the slack on the home and parenting front. And the weeks that he has a higher work load (he is a chef, so that depends on the week or if there are special events going on, like Restaurant Week), then the rolls reverse, and I pick up the slack. We have made a great team because we communicate well, and I keep a very detailed schedule noting what is going on each week.

When it comes to parenting and having the multitude of jobs/ clients that I have, it hasn't always been easy, especially when I was a single parent working nine different jobs and in grad school full-time. That two years of my life is a bit of a blur, and I didn't sleep much. I probably didn't spend as much time with my kids as I would have liked to, either, but I did everything I could to work when they were sleeping or not with me. Hence, the low level of sleep for two years on my end.

Even now, as a blended family, I do my best to get up at the ass crack of dawn (sometimes as early as 3:00 a.m.) to get work done before it's time for the day to begin with the kids. As a parent, I know my time with the kids is limited. My oldest will be fourteen this year, so he will be gone before I know it. And I will never get this time back, so if it means sacrifice on my part, with regard to sleep, then that is what needs to be done. So, for now, I work early mornings and while they are in school. Once I pick up the oldest from school, at 2:15 p.m., I spend one-on-one time with him before I have to leave to pick up the other kids. And I wouldn't trade this time with him for anything.

Being a parent and working, no matter how diverse your skill set or your workload, means something has to give sometimes. You have to learn to be creative with your time and your energy. Being this diverse throughout my life has helped me learn how to juggle things more effec- tively and not let the balls drops. So, all in all, this level of diversity has only increased my skills as an effective parent—most days, that is. If you are a parent, you will understand that not all days are a win. Some days are better than others, but don't beat yourself up about it. Just vow to have a better day tomorrow by learning from your mistakes today and vowing to be a better version of yourself as each day passes. At least, that is what I try to do each and every day. And so far, the kids seem to enjoy having me as a parent. Hell, some of them still follow me around to the bathroom, so I must be doing something right!

Now that you have learned a little bit about me and how I operate, I want to delve into the different jobs that have created this high level of diversity you see before you. But first, I want to note that this lifestyle may not be for everyone. Yes, we are all capable of pushing ourselves outside of our comfort zone and learning new things, but some of us live in a bit more fear than others, with regard to change. Not only that but some of us have a much more difficult time balancing multiple things at once. I'm not saying that either of these are bad personality traits, so please don't take offense if you happen to fit into one of these categories. If you do, it just means you will have to move at a slower pace with your level of diversity. You may also only be comfortable enough to handle two different skill sets at one time, as opposed to the multitude I am suggesting. You know you better than anyone else in the world, so you should only incorporate what you think you can effectively handle, while still being efficient and enjoying your life. If you get to a point where you have crossed the line into stress and unhappiness, then dialing it down until you cross back over the line to happiness is the best way to go. This goes for everybody because there is always a fine line between loving your life and hating it. Find the line and ride it!

# Introduction

L ife seems to be full of neat little boxes, which everything and everyone is supposed to fit into. It appears these little boxes, and the things that fit into them, are the only source of sanity the majority of us have. I, personally, have always hated these little boxes and do everything in my power to break out of them at every given opportunity. I find that it throws people off, shakes up their world, and gets them to think OUTSIDE of the predetermined boxes. Yes, I like to rock the boat. A LOT! Not because I like to irritate others but because it's who I am. I was born as a healer, a game changer, a therapist, a person who makes people think about things from a different perspective. Due to that, not even my job history is considered normal, nor would I ever want it to be.

I have been called many things in my life, related to my work history. Not all of them are necessarily deemed a good thing. The two that stick out the most are "Jack of All Trades" and "The Jamaican." Now the former seems to make mountains of sense, as you will soon see. However, the latter I always had a hard time grasping simply because I don't understand the reference or why they would call me that. What this all breaks down to is that I have always had a multitude of jobs at a time, sometimes up to ten. People seem to give me strange looks more often than not because of all the things I have done in so many different fields. I suppose I don't quite understand why this is such a foreign concept to the majority of people I've run across because I feel like life is short and meant to be experienced. What better way to experience it, besides taking off and traveling the entire world (which is my main goal in life) than to work in as many different fields as you can, to get a better understanding of the way other people think and how the world works. Seeing as this is not how most people live, though, maybe I can understand their confused looks. Of course, sometimes, this also makes it much harder for me to find a job because my experience is not based on years in the same field but rather being all over the place. A lot of potential employers hate this and won't even give me a second look, even though I'm a very fast learner and very adaptable. I may not ever be the best in any field, but I can usually become very good at what I do, and that's when I get bored and abandon ship for something else to stimulate me further. I just love the experience of life and want to experience as much of it as I can! The only way I have found to keep me interested in one particular job once I've figured out its nuances is to work another job at the same time that is completely different. This works different parts of my brain, keeps me on my toes, and keeps me interested longer. So let's start at the beginning and work up to the present.

# LAYING THE FOUNDATION

# Babysitting

The first job I ever had that was paid, besides chores at home, of course, was babysitting the neighborhood kids. At the age of fourteen, I started babysitting some of the children on the same block as us. I babysat for a few different families occasionally, but one family I watched on a regular basis, the Williamses. Lauren and her little brother, Michael, to be more specific. Lauren was four and Michael was almost two when I started watching them. They had very different looks, yet you could tell they were siblings. Lauren was a dainty little blond, with big inquisitive eyes, and Michael had black hair and blue eyes. The two of them did what siblings always do, *fight!* But we had a great time playing together. I watched them mostly during the day so their mother could run errands without them while her husband was at work. Now, as a single mother of two, I fully understand this. I am very grateful for the time they are with their father because that is when I get the most done. Children are fantastic, but they can make doing everyday chores and errands much more difficult. Until I had children, I took going to the grocery store alone for granted, which I will never do again!

That time with Lauren and Michael was probably one of my best "work" memories. The reason being is because it didn't really feel like work most of the time. I was getting paid to play with these two energetic and curious children. They asked lots of questions which I thoroughly enjoyed because I loved being able to answer them when I could and find the answers when I couldn't. Now this was before the internet, so I didn't have Google to rely on. I had to use those things they call books and libraries to find answers I didn't know. Seeing as I have always had a thirst for knowledge, though, this was a great experience for me in problem-solving. The kids loved it when I came back with an answer to their questions, but then, of course, they would have about a million more on the subject after that! This was definitely training me for motherhood because my children ask a ridiculous amount of questions on a fairly regular basis. Except now, I have Google to fall back on instead of going to the library!

1

**What I Learned**

★   How to multitask with children of different ages

★   How to be creative with food, to get children to eat

★   How to read a story with cool voices

★   How to sit through the *same* movie over, and over, and over again

★   How to coddle a child enough to get them to sleep

★   How to manage multiple children at a pool

# First Real Job

My first real job after babysitting was working for The Limited Too. Which I believe is now called Justice. One of my best friends, Erin, had just gotten a job there at the mall and told me I should come and work with her there. At the age of fifteen, I wasn't quite old enough to work here without a work permit, or to drive myself. So I went and got a work permit, and my dad used to drive me to and from work. Erin and I had a great time working at this clothing store, most of the time. Our direct manager was a woman named Robin, whom I still remember well today. She didn't seem to be as fond of us teenyboppers but tolerated us as much as she could. However, since we were working in a children and pre-teen's clothing store, we fit pretty well. I remember the clothing style then was much different than it is now; this was the mid 90s, after all. There were leggings but more actual jeans than are currently in stores. The shirts were not nearly as belly-showing and skimpy as they are today, either. The music was also much different than today's music playing in clothing stores. It was a lot of upbeat 50s music that was playing on the Musak. I always thought of being at a soda shop or a sock hop when I was there, although I am not old enough to have ever been at either. I made somewhere around $7 an hour at this—my first real job. After Erin and I got exhausted with this job, and being harassed by Robin, we both quit. I believe I worked there a total of eight months.

★ How to merchandise effectively for maximum sales

★ How rude people are when it comes to leaving clothes all over the dressing room

★ How to handle opposing personalities and aggression

★ How to interface with customers and create a sale

★ How to upsell

★ How to take inventory

★ How to cold call

★ How to listen to the same oldies Musak over and over again without losing my mind!

# Still at the Mall

I found a job at The Cookie Store, upstairs in the same mall, before I quit The Limited Too, however. My father always told me to make sure I had another job lined up before I quit one because it's much easier to *find* a job when you already *have* a job. I have continued to abide by this logic into my adult life and have found it to be generally 100% true. At this job, I worked with another high school friend, Tina. She and I had a really good time at this place! Our direct manager was a skinny redhead named Steve who was in his early to mid twenties. His boss was a man named Jeff who was rarely ever there. When he was, though, you could cut the tension with a knife. Looking back now, I see this was because he was trying to run a business, and all of the teenagers and slacker managers were not doing their best to make sure his business succeeded. Back then, however, I saw him almost as a tyrant. Funny how time and experience changes one's perspective on things.

I enjoyed this job for the short time I was there—primarily because I got to create cookie cakes in the back of the store. The other main perk was that I got to people-watch at the mall. We all had a lot of fun playing and joking around behind the scenes. I have to admit, though, when Jeff wasn't there to oversee us, we rarely got any real work done, and Steve gave away a lot of cookies to women he was attracted to. All of those things didn't bode well for Jeff and his profit/loss margins, so one day in the middle of summer, he ended up getting rid of all of us, including Steve. This was a short-lived job for me, but one that taught me to really be my own person and stick with the work ethic that had been instilled in me, as well as not getting too caught up in the surrounding antics.

★ How to make a cookie cake from hundreds of mini cookies

★ How to stage food to make it more appealing to potential customers

★ How to schedule a small staff

★ How to take special orders and execute them in the time allotted

★ To listen to my gut and not just go with the flow because it may end up biting me in the ass!

# Italian Oven

Afriend my job at The Cookie Store ended, I took a very small break and then jumped right back into working. I found a small Italian restaurant closer to my parents' house called the Italian Oven, and applied there. I got the job as a hostess upon handing in my application. The environment was low-key, family-fun Italian food that was created in an open kitchen layout with a wood-burning oven. Seating customers was a very simple job for me to grasp. Although, I did get trained on their computer system called a POS (Point of Sale) which was a much higher tech version of what I had been using at The Cookie Store. This POS was more than just a glorified calculator, which is what I was used to. It actually performed all of the functions necessary to make a sale, as well as the required math and taxes. I had to use a pass code to unlock it, as opposed to an old-fashioned key. If it weren't for all of the buttons being labeled on the keypad, I wouldn't know what to enter. At least this was something new for me to learn, but I realized, after not too long, the POS came by its nickname, "Piece of Shit," quite honestly. For all of its functionality, it still had regular glitches, so everything had to be double and triple checked for accuracy.

Even though I enjoyed learning something new, I quickly bored of seating families and hanging out at the hostess stand, waiting for customers to possibly purchase any of our assorted signature Italian Oven items. I asked if I could please train to be a server so I could not only make more money but learn a new skill. As soon as I turned sixteen, they began letting me train to serve tables. I liked that portion of this particular job more than being a hostess because I got to interact more with the families, plus I made more money. I have to say, though, any time I hear that horribly clichéd Italian-style song that has the lyrics, "When the moon hits your eye, like a big pizza pie, that's amore!" it takes me back to that restaurant. Not only did it play incessantly, but we had to sing a Happy Birthday song to our birthday guests with a butchered version of that song.

The atmosphere there began to change for me after a few months, and especially after I got a job at Crowley's as a hostess and felt the energy at that restaurant. I realized there was a looming underlying sexual current running at the Italian Oven, and although I felt it, I didn't fully realize how dangerous it could be until it directly affected me. I had worked there for about six months, and the manager, Bill, was a regular flirt with all of the girls that were in his employ. I didn't think anything of it, really, except that I generally tried to avoid him whenever I could, so as to avoid his stare or off-color comments. He bothered the older girls more than he did me, but that changed after I started working at Crowley's. I don't know if he felt there was a threat of me leaving the IO completely, or if he decided that he would push the envelope with me and see how far he could get. I remember going into his office to get my paycheck one afternoon, and he asked me to shut the door because he needed to speak with me. I did as he asked but felt uncomfortable about the situation. He asked me if I would like a raise. I told him that, of course, I would. He then proceeded to tell me he would be more than willing to give somebody like me a raise if I would do some "favors" for him. He told me I was a very beautiful girl and that I was someone everybody fantasized about. And he would love to help me if I helped him. I told him no thank you, that I wasn't interested. I took my paycheck and left, and I never went back.

**4**

**What I Learned**

★ How to seat tables in an organized manner

★ How to take orders using shorthand

★ How to take orders without writing anything down

★ How to use a POS system to input merchandise, food and drink orders

★ How to deliver food and beverages to a table without spilling anything

★ How to connect with my tables to get better tips

★ How NOT to put up with sexual harassment and walk away

# Crowley's Stonehenge/ Crowley's Courtyard/ 5 Points Pub

I got recommended as a hostess at this restaurant down the street named Crowley's. Now the three owners happened to own three restaurants in the Raleigh area with the same name. The one at Stonehenge was the closest to my house, and Erin was one of my good friends. So when she told me about the restaurant, and how much she liked it and the crew, I applied. They hired me on the spot, via word of mouth, and I began to hostess.

I got to wear nicer clothes and not just a uniform, which I really enjoyed. I learned their seating system, as well as the system in the bar and lounge with the cocktail tables. I agreed with her wholeheartedly, in that I really liked the staff there. Most of the staff were in their younger twenties or late teens, like us. The general manager, Barry, and his sidekick, Rich, were pretty cool dudes.

Now I can't say there wasn't a sexual undercurrent running in that place either because there certainly was and is, in every form of food service I have been in. However, these guys had a little bit more respect for the younger staff and weren't overt about it. There was harmless flirting but nothing aggressive, like in my previous job.

After hostessing for a few months, they let me begin to train as a server. Just as before, I made more money as a server and began to create a regular clientele. I worked not only dinners but lunches and sometimes straight through doubles. Those were long days, especially with still being in school, but I learned a lot about how to hustle and multitask, as well as how to run on little sleep. This latter quality I already had, but I just learned how to fine-tune it when I was there.

Once I turned eighteen, I began to cocktail waitress in the bar and lounge, and this is where I first learned how to bartend. Now, please don't mistake this for saying that I bartended at the age of eighteen, but the bartenders taught me how to make drinks, and I served them. I learned what the drinks were and what was in them, as well as which regulars liked what types of drinks.

I began to collect a regular clientele on this side of the restaurant, as well, but the clients on this side had a tendency to tip more. It got to the point where I could recommend drinks to guests based on what they told me their likes were. I still do this today whenever I bartend, which isn't as much as it has been in previous years. To me, bartending is an art, just like cooking and baking, with science thrown in for good measure. If you understand the chemistry of flavors and people's tastes, and how things look aesthetically, you can create pretty much anything eye-catching and palatable to anyone.

It was also at this time that I started getting more creative in that, if a guest told me it was their birthday, or they were celebrating something and begged me for a drink on the house, I would tell them, "Most certainly!" I would then bring them a blow job shot and make them take it. Everybody loved this, and I got really big tips when I did things like this. Although, doing things like this also requires being able to read someone's personality, to see if this type of behavior is something that would make the experience more enjoyable and memorable or offend them.

After some time at just the Stonehenge location, they asked me if I could come over and work lunches and some dinners at the Edwards Mill location, as well. I began to do that and didn't like the energy or the management at that location nearly as much. I worked at that location for a little over a year, just filling in, when I wasn't working at Stonehenge or some of my other jobs.

The owners also owned a bar in the downtown Raleigh area called 5 Points Pub, and they asked if I could please bartend there a couple nights a week. I began adding that to my repertoire. That crew was a skeleton crew (a bare-bones staff necessary for only the basic operation of a business to stay up and running, but nothing more than that) at that point, but I enjoyed it. The biggest issue I had with that particular location was that I had to close up by myself at 2:00 a.m. There were a few other bars nearby and two gas stations, but I had to park my car down the back alley, and I was always alone upon closing.

At this time, I had been harassed and followed a few times, so I felt rightly concerned and went out to get a concealed carry permit. I had been involved and practiced the original Thailand form of kickboxing, Muay Thai, but thought the added level of protection may come in handy at some point. I went with friends to learn to shoot but never actually went through with the purchase of a firearm. It came in handy that I was dating a Raleigh Police Department (RPD) police officer for part of my stent at 5 Points because, when he worked the night shift, he would park his cruiser across the street from me and keep an eye on me when I was closing.

The neighborhood around 5 Points Pub had been trying to shut the bar down for years because they didn't like the late-night bands or the loud drunks that came in there regularly, so they put together an undercover sting operation. Luckily for me, this was not with Alcohol Law Enforcement (ALE) but with RPD. At the time the sting happened, we had gotten so much negative feedback from the neighborhood that a lot of the regulars had stopped coming, and we were down to the older men in the area because the younger crowd had moved further downtown where there were less issues.

I was working by myself on a Sunday afternoon, with only a few of the older gentlemen in as patrons. A younger guy walked in—which was odd but did happen every now and then—and ordered a beer. I didn't card him because, as previously mentioned, the younger crowd had moved on. He said that he was waiting for a friend of his and sat down with the beer. He never actually drank any of it, and then he asked if he could go outside to make a phone call and see where his friend was. I told him that was perfectly fine. The next thing I know, I have the younger guy and a slightly older guy standing in front of me, telling me I have just been busted for serving a minor. I asked them if they were serious and have they taken a look around at the crowd? Nobody that is under age would choose to patronize this bar. Since it was RPD, he gave me a court date and said that I would have to take a class on serving minors, and then it would be expunged (which it is), but I had to tell my boss.

My boss wasn't pleased, but he also knew the place was on the way out because of all the negative feedback from the neighborhood (which I, in fact, learned in court was the reason for the sting operation, and the RPD officer who busted me wasn't thrilled about it, especially after all his buddies gave him crap in the courtroom for busting me). My boss told me I was lucky it was RPD and not ALE putting the sting together because, if ALE had done it, their license could have been pulled for everything they owned, and I would be considered off limits to be a bartender in this town.

The class was a one-day, ridiculously easy class on how to discern a real license from a fake license, which I already knew, and they reiterated how important it was to check for ID every time. I was one of the only bartenders in the class, as everyone else was busted for selling cigarettes to minors. A few months after I took this class, I was informed we were going to be shutting down the bar for good and that I would work the farewell shift.

This happened in April of 2000, and I continued to work for Crowley's until June of 2001, when I got a real full-time job and stopped waiting tables for a while. The six-year experience I had with these restaurants and the owners ended up teaching me a great deal of things about myself and my character, as well as shaping more of my work ethic today. Whenever I think back on these years in my life, it is always with fondness.

5

**What I Learned**

★ How to hostess in a faster paced environment

★ How to wash dishes

★ How to prep food

★ How to work double shifts and still be awake and friendly

★ How to be a cocktail waitress in a bar

★ How to bartend

★ How to get more creative with my drink offerings, to increase my sales and tips

★ How to create new drinks out of thin air based on what customers told me they liked

★ How to run a bar by myself at night

★ How to change a keg

★ How to not get busted for serving alcohol to a minor

★ How much influence people can have on an establishment and its survival

★ How to schedule and deal with vendors

# Papa John's Raleigh

I got another job at Papa John's right around the same time as I started Crowley's, due to yet another friend, Tina, who worked there and told me they needed help. Now, as a person with Celiac Disease, you would think this wasn't the wisest option, but me being a know-it-all teenager meant that, at this time in my life, I thought I knew more than the doctors did. This is especially true because Celiac was still not widely known then, and very few people even knew what I was talking about. Therefore, I knew more than the experts. You have just got to love how the teenage brain operates sometimes and wonder how any of us survive to adulthood! But I digress. They hired me on the spot, due to Tina's recommendation, as well. This was before computer operated anything, so we had to handwrite all orders on paper slips and hang them on the line for the crew to make. I took orders to begin with, which was pretty easy, especially because there weren't any computers for me to screw up. Not very long after I started, though, they asked me if I wanted to learn how to make pizzas. I, of course, said yes. In case you haven't noticed yet, I have a tendency to pick things up fairly quickly and then bore of them, which then requires me to learn a new skill. If this doesn't happen, then I move on. I learned how to knead and toss pizza dough, to give it its shape, and how to spread the sauce on correctly. I then learned how they liked the toppings to go on the pies, with the toppings being underneath the cheese. I thought this was pretty cool because every other pizza place put the cheese on and then the toppings. After I learned how to do all of this, the GM taught me how to take inventory and order products. I started doing that regularly with Tina because the GM started to become increasingly absent and unreliable with regard to when and if he came into work. We figured out later that he had a drinking problem and possibly a drug problem, so we had become the honorary Assistant Managers. We helped with the schedule and called people in when we were short-staffed. We basically did everything he was supposed to do because he wasn't doing it. This wasn't hard for me to figure out, and I liked the responsibility, as well as gaining the resourcefulness in problem-solving.

**What I Learned**

6

★    How to properly toss pizza dough

★    How to take orders by hand

★    How to schedule drivers by route

★    How to take inventory at higher volume

★    How to place orders with vendors for product

★    How to balance a till properly

★    How to manage a store when your GM is MIA

# Manchester's

This job was another one I got through the same friend that got me the job at Crowley's. The owner of this restaurant happened to be good friends and drinking buddies with one of the owners of Crowley's, which is how he happened upon recruiting my friend to work for him, also. After she had worked there for a few months, she asked me if I wanted to work there, also, since I could use more money and wanted more diversity. I, once again, got hired on site and began waiting tables for him at his Italian-style restaurant. It was a little higher scale than Crowley's, so the crowd and the technique was a bit different, which I liked. Sadly, I can't tell you a whole lot about this job other than I learned how to fold napkins in different shapes, and that the staff was exceptionally snotty and stuck up, in my book. I didn't stay with him for longer than a few months because I didn't appreciate his managerial style, which entailed yelling and screaming how lazy and horrible we were as employees. I learned then and there that I do not like, or handle well, a manager that exhibits the New Jersey style of management that was rampant in the 80s. Anytime I've run across a supervisor with this management style, I have done my best to make a hasty exit.

★ How to fold napkins into fancy shapes

★ How to deal with New Jersey management style personalities

★ How to know when enough is enough and that some things are just not worth it for me

# FRAMING THE HOUSE

# Angiosonics

This was the first job I had outside of the food and beverage industry which was the summer between my Junior and Senior year of high school, and then, again, the summer after I graduated, until I went away to college. My father worked for this medical technology device company, and they needed a receptionist. This was a startup in the USA but run out of another country. I got to work in a large office in Research Triangle Park (RTP) and found the technology they were creating and working with to be extremely interesting. This company had created a product which could be inserted through the thigh and up into the heart, to break up clots using a balloon to depress the clots. Just watching the test cases, as well as helping in any way I could, really helped me to see that I wanted to do something more to help people, as opposed to merely serving food for the rest of my life. While I was with this company, I learned not only how to answer phones professionally but how to implement and incorporate an organized filing system—a skill which I have utilized tirelessly in the subsequent years. I learned about capacitors, resistors, diodes, motherboards, probes, and more about how the human body worked. This job was really the first one to challenge me and put me outside of my comfort zone, in the sense that I learned a lot of information in a short period of time. This position also taught me about how corporate organizations are structured, which has been another asset to me throughout the years. I may not have been that important in the grand scheme of things, in this position, but I was a wheel in the cog that helped move the whole machine, and for that, I am always grateful.

★ How to work in a corporate environment

★ How to be even *more* organized

★ How the medical device industry works

★ How the corporate chain of command works

★ How certain parts of a computer operate and why they are necessary

# RJ Gator's

This restaurant was my shortest stint at any job I can recall. I was going to college in Wilmington, North Carolina at the time and decided right before winter break of my freshman year to get a job for side money. RJ Gators was right down the street from campus, and they needed a hostess. I wanted to wait tables because there is more money there, but they told me I would have to be a hostess to learn the menu and tables first, and then they would move me up to server in a short period of time. The menu here was much different than I had seen before, in the sense that they had things on it like alligator and crawdads. The menu was a little more difficult for me to learn because of its diversity, but I enjoyed the challenge, even if I couldn't eat any of the food to describe to patrons. This was an extremely easy job, and the environment was very laid back, to boot. I went home for winter break, and when I came back, the restaurant had been closed, and a new establishment was in the works, Pure Gold, the gentlemen's club. They offered every employee of RJ Gator's a job at Pure Gold and told me I could be a shot girl, but I was really not interested in that type of job at all, primarily because my parents would have killed me. Hence, the end of that position with RJ Gator's.

★ How to use a different POS

★ How to learn a more diverse menu

★ How to roll with the punches of life

# Papa John's Wilmington

While I was in Wilmington, in college, I began working for Papa John's again. I did the same things as I did in Raleigh, with regards to making pies and helping with inventory, but I also began to help them with the marketing in the area, by putting out fliers and going door to door (this was before the internet was widely used for anything more than dial-up AOL).

This was my first experience going door to door for anything, and I can't say it was really my preference. Once a week, I would go into the office, grab a ton of flyers, and talk to my boss about what area I was thinking about hitting. He wanted me to stick to only our delivery area when I passed flyers out, so that narrowed down where I would have to drive. I didn't get paid mileage for this, either, by the way, which didn't make this aspect of the job any more attractive.

One thing I didn't realize, at first, was that I was not supposed to be putting flyers in anybody's mailbox. Apparently, that is against the law, and any person or company breaching it could get into some major trouble. That should have been disclosed to me *before* I ever started passing out flyers. Luckily, though, I didn't get caught before I was informed of this law, after only a few times of breaking it. Then I had to switch tactics and actually start going up to each door and talking to the homeowner. I got a lot of doors slammed in my face, as you can imagine. Especially for somebody only trying to pass out pizza coupons. I mean, damn, everybody likes pizza!

The other step I began to take was to put the flyers on car windshields while they were in parking lots. Now, as an adult, I really hate it when people do this to my car, so it's probably pizza karma coming back to haunt me. I can't tell you whether any of these flyer tactics actually worked for the company because they never disclosed any information to me with regards to marketing or revenue. But I did my job, and they paid me for it, which was the whole reason why I was there.

I worked for this company, all in all, for three years, which was long enough for me. While I added some new skills to my basket, I also learned that somebody with Celiac really shouldn't be around all of the flour, nor be eating pizza. This experience made me realize that, as much as I wanted to not have Celiac anymore and just fit in, I do have it, and there are certain things that are in my best interest to avoid. Copious amounts of flour just happens to be a big one! So, I decided, in the best interest of my health, to exit that place of employment.

★ How to go door to door and solicit (everybody loves this skill!)

★ How to organize my time to be the most efficient

★ How college students aren't usually smarter than doctors!

# Eddie Romanelli's

While in Wilmington, I picked up a job as a server at yet another Italian restaurant (do you see a pattern here?) called Eddie Romanelli's. This restaurant was part of a chain of three different restaurants in the area, all with different food fare. This was the most upscale restaurant I had worked in, ever, in the sense that I had to wear a white button-down collared shirt, with black pants and a tie. Everything had white tablecloths and cloth napkins, and I learned more about wine and presentation at this place of employment.

We had to go to regular tastings for the food and beverages, as well as had regular testing on the menu, before we were allowed to serve. I was in training for almost a full month at this position before I was allowed to have my own section. This was the most difficult part for me because the menu was so vast, as was the wine menu.

I spent a lot of time shadowing the strongest servers, in a rotating fashion. They each had different tricks and tips for remembering the menu and the wines. What worked the best for me was to spend some time in the kitchen, to see how they plated each dish. Since each dish was unique, this process made it easier for me to memorize the menu based on the ingredients.

The wine was harder for me to memorize because I wasn't twenty-one yet and hadn't really developed a palate for wine (unless it was boxed White Zinfandel, and I don't think that counts). But the restaurant was very big on making sure we knew what paired well with what, so we spent a lot of time going over each wine and its unique characteristics. This was really my first in-depth lesson into wine and jargon such as legs, body, tannins, fruit forward, and nose. I took the wine list home, along with the associated document that went into great depth about each individual wine. I played a matching game with myself when I first started working on memorizing the wine list.

Once I got the matching game down, I took it up a notch and hid the in-depth descriptions of the wines. This meant I had nothing to look at and had to just pull the information out of my brain. I tried to visualize the dishes that went well with each wine in my head so I had a positive correlation between wines and food.

By the time I had to take the wine test, which was about a month in, I passed with flying colors. This was probably my favorite part—and the hardest part—of this job, since it was a new skill I didn't previously have.

One of my least favorite parts was having to help out in the dish pit, which was not something I had to really partake in before. We were constantly understaffed, and in typical restaurant fashion, the dishwasher would just not show up some days. There wasn't a golden rule with regard to who had to jump into the dish pit when we were busy on days the dishwasher didn't show, but I volunteered more than a few times. This is not because I *wanted* to hang out in the dish pit, but because it needed to get done, and it wasn't something I had done before, so I was willing to give it a try. Cleaning out the traps in the dishwasher is absolutely disgusting, and I wouldn't wish it on anybody, but it taught me a lesson in humility. It also taught me just how much work is involved in running a dish pit, effectively and efficiently, and how underappreciated dishwashers are. From this job on, I had a new respect for the people who wash dishes, and I always did my best to remember to tip them out, also. After all, if it wasn't for the dishwasher, none of us would have clean dishes to serve our food on to customers. They are important!

I wasn't at this job for an extremely long time, but I felt like I really grew as a server because of this position. It made me pay more attention to detail and taught me how to properly pair wine with dishes, which I am grateful for. Overall, it was a good experience, and I wouldn't trade it. The money here was really good, by my standards, but it was the highest level of memorization that I had to maintain regularly.

**11**

**What I Learned**

★ How to differentiate wines on a wine list

★ How to sell wines based on the likes of a customer

★ How to clean out a dishwasher (disgusting!)

★ How to step up my level of service from two- and three-star to four-star service

# Seagate Fire Department

**D**uring the end of my freshman year in college, I started casually dating a guy who had a few roommates. One of the roommates was a firefighter who worked near the college at a volunteer fire station. He approached me about it one day, to see if I was interested. I was surprised he approached me about it at all, but I did stop to think about the possibilities. I had never really considered being a firefighter but, since the opportunity had presented itself, why the hell not give it a shot. I told him I would stop by one day in the next week to check out the station. He told me I didn't even really have to apply because they were trying to diversify and wanted to bring on some women.

When I went into the station the next week, he gave me the grand tour of Seagate, and I met most of the guys. The station was nice, as were all of the crew members. Before I could leave, Chiefee (Assistant Fire Captain) asked me if I was interested and, if so, to wait so they could take a vote on my behalf. Longer story short, they voted me in. I was given my turnout gear and my helmet and assigned number 724. At this point in time, volunteer firefighters got paid, but not nearly as much as full-time firefighters with the city. But I certainly didn't argue with getting paid!

This whole two years was a very interesting and memorable experience for me, as it was something completely different than I had ever done. We did have regular trainings and certifications that we had to get. These were scheduled with other stations in the Wilmington area so that we could all collaborate, get to know each other, and streamline the classes offered.

During one of the larger training sessions, which was a weekend event, we all were instructed to take as many classes in our areas of interest we could get for credit hours. I remember learning a ton of information that weekend but found that I had one area I really liked. I took a class on HAZMAT placards that taught us what hazardous materials were, how to fight a fire that may include them, and how to read placards on trucks that indicated them. I absolutely loved this class, and from that point on, I made that my area of study.

One of my favorite memories is when we got to "play" in a donated house. We did multiple training exercises including chopping down the door, egress exercises, hauling dummies out with our full turnout gear on, and using the Jaws of Life on a few donated cars on the property. I can recall just how difficult it was for me, swinging the ax inside that house, trying to tear through the wall. I am, and was, a fairly fit person. But legs are my strong suit. My arms are more in line with a typical female's arm strength, so this was an immense challenge, and I was sore for days afterwards! The Jaws of Life weren't any different, as those suckers are HEAVY!

We were also taught how to break a car window without shattering it—in case a victim was still inside—with a punch and some duct tape. This is funny to me because it stuck in my head, and I still know how to do it. In case of some freak emergency where I need to haul somebody out of a car, and just happen to have a punch and a roll of duct tape on me!

For the most part, Wilmington was pretty quiet, so we didn't get a whole lot of actual fire action. But I will never forget my first time in a fire. I don't think anyone ever does.

We got a call that a trailer not too far from the university was fully engulfed. Luckily, this trailer park was close to our station, and we were there and not out on a food-run. As soon as we arrived, the leads started to go in with the hose. Shawn, a co-worker who sort of took me under his training wing, so to speak, stayed with me and told me to get the rest of my turnout gear on. I put everything on and made sure my SCBA (Self Contained Breathing Apparatus) was functioning properly. This is the most vital part of the turnout gear, in my mind, because it is what provides your oxygen and keeps you alive.

I grabbed on to the hose after Shawn and went into the blackness. I remember how hot and stuffy it felt. If I were a claustrophobic person, this would not have worked for me at all because it felt like being trapped in a pit of stifling blackness.

I reminded myself to stay calm and just breathe. We were looking for potential victims, and that was all that mattered. We had made it through the first part of the house and were heading toward the kitchen when my SCBA stopped working. At first, I thought it was just me panicking, but I had been calm, so that didn't correlate in my brain. After a few seconds of trying to get some fresh air, I realized I wasn't getting anything, and then I started to panic. I reached out in front of me and yanked on Shawn's arm. As he turned to look at me, I motioned to my SCBA, with a panicked look on my face. He turned fully around and started guiding me out of the house with the hose.

As soon as we made it back outside, I started ripping my gear off so I could get some oxygen. I felt like I was going to vomit all over the grass. After basically hyperventilating to get oxygen into my lungs, he left me and went back in to continue the search. There were other fellow firefighters outside manning the truck and plenty of onlookers, which made the situation that much more embarrassing for me. After all, this was my first time going into a fire, and I had to leave because my gear malfunctioned. In all reality, we found out later that whoever had used this tank last forgot to charge it, so it was low on oxygen. This is a standard operating procedure upon return from any call where the SCBA's are used, or at least it was at the time. They are all supposed to be charged and replaced on the truck so that everything is full and ready to go. *But,* each time you are dispatched to a call, you are supposed to double-check your gear to make sure everything is in order, and I didn't fully get that yet, so that was a failure on my end.

Overall, everyone survived. I lived and learned a very valuable lesson. *Always, always* check your gear! This follows true in any job.

While at 5 Points, if I had only checked the license of the guy trying to buy a pint from me (which was my job), then I wouldn't have found myself in court for serving alcohol to a minor. I found myself in hot water because I didn't double-check something that could have ultimately been a much bigger disaster than it ended up being.

This is where double-checking comes into play in so many ways. Luckily for me! It is like that old adage in the building industry that states, "Measure twice and cut once." Basically, double check everything!

After we put the fire out, we found the PO (Point of Origin) to be the stove in the kitchen. The woman who was renting the trailer was a single mother of two who was attending the university. She was apparently making French fries for her children as part of the dinner, on the stove in oil, and left to go back to the store to get something else. Well, she left the stove on, and that was the end of that. They lost everything. But they all walked away alive. So, in all reality, even though I am sure this was a very difficult time for her, she learned a really important lesson, and so did I. This is one that has stuck with me throughout the years. Whenever I think that things are bad, I remember the looks on this family's faces, and I know it could always be worse.

After that fire, I actually didn't have very many in the subsequent two years I was with the department. We did end up doing a lot of evacuations, due to weather, which made up the bulk of our workload. Of course, that's beside sitting around the station, cooking in the kitchen and watching NASCAR. I swear to all that is holy that I had to try every single day I was there not to poke my eyeballs out. I have never been a NASCAR fan. And to each their own, but I have never understood why anybody wants to sit around and watch a bunch of cars drive around in a circle a few hundred times. In order to keep my sanity, I hung out in the kitchen, cooking or working on schoolwork most of the time when we weren't doing training exercises or out on calls.

I did get to learn how to drive the truck, though, which was pretty cool but scary as hell. I was always worried that I was going to take somebody out on accident. The biggest rule of thumb, as a first responder, is that you must not create other incidents on your way to an incident. Luckily, I never had to drive the truck to any calls. But I did drive it frequently to Home Depot, Dairy Queen, and Subway. Parking that beast was a nightmare!

Overall, I really enjoyed this experience and everything I learned while I was with the department. I ended up leaving the station when I moved back to Raleigh. A bunch of the guys asked me if I was going to join a station in Raleigh because they would vouch for me. I told them I appreciated it, and really enjoyed the experience, but that it was time for me to move on.

**12**

**What I Learned**

★ How to use the Jaws of Life

★ How to break down a wall with an ax

★ How to clear a house

★ How to evacuate a community during severe weather

★ How to properly use turnout gear and an SCBA

★ How to drive a fire truck without killing anyone

★ What a HAZMAT placard is and how to differentiate them

# Communities in Schools

While I was in Wilmington at UNCW, I found another program where I could be of use. This was a volunteer program, similar to the fire department, except that this one didn't pay anything for my services. I had first been introduced to this program when I was a senior in high school and worked with other local kids that were younger than I.

This program pairs high school and/or college students with other younger children that come from a troubled past. What that really means is that the mentee that the mentor is paired with is somebody who is not doing great in school, usually due to outside circumstances. The goal is for the mentor (me) to be there for the mentee in any way possible to get them back on track.

Sometimes, the mentor helps with homework or school projects, and other times, the mentor is just there to help get the other student out of their situation for a little while and help them reset. I did the latter, mostly, by taking my mentees to the park, or to get ice cream, or to a movie, or to the beach. I would just let them talk and get off their chests whatever was bothering them. Frequently, this helped them get back into the frame of mind they needed to be in so they could focus on their schoolwork.

Unfortunately, I don't recall the names of the mentees I had in the program, but I had three different girls throughout my duration as a mentor. I recall that one of them was a foster child and had a lot of anger issues. She was in middle school and was failing everything. I did my best to work with her on increasing her grades, but it became too tumultuous once she threatened to steal my car. So I asked to be reassigned.

The second one—the one I had the longest—lived with some family members because she and her sister had been removed from their mother's custody. I don't remember why, exactly, but the aunt she lived with was pretty vocal about what a horrible person the mother was. This mentee and I worked really well together for many months, and her grades increased, which was the goal. She opened up to me, and we really started to forge a relationship. As a human and a natural problem-solver, I felt for her and just wanted to help her become the best version of herself. The last day I spent with her, she was very upset about her mother and one of their other siblings that was still residing with her mother. She asked me if there was any way I could take her to see them where they lived in Southport. I told her no, many times, but I eventually caved and told her that I would so she could get some resolution and try to move on. In hindsight, this was the completely wrong thing to do, and I should have stuck by my initial gut response. But I didn't, so I am ultimately responsible.

I took her to see her mother and other sibling. They all talked outside, and I stayed with her the whole time. After being there for almost an hour, I told her we had to go so that I could bring her back to her aunt's house. When we got there, the aunt questioned what had taken us so long to return. I told her the truth, and she exploded. She told me to say goodbye to her niece and that I would never get to see her again. Both my mentee and myself were upset and crying because we had reached a point where we had a connection, or at least that is how I felt about it at the time.

I received a call the next day from my boss in the program and was informed that I was being pulled off of her case and being reassigned. I was warned that, should I do something of that caliber again, I would no longer be welcome in the program. My oversight to the brevity of the situation was highly embarrassing to me, as I should have known better. Since this experience, I have made a very conscious effort to listen more closely to my gut instinct and pause before I make a decision.

My last mentee was in elementary school and had been having a hard time being bullied. She was in foster care, as well. This child was very sweet and loving, and we made a lot of art together. Her biggest issue in school was that she had an extremely hard time with language and spelling. So we worked on this regularly, usually while sitting at an ice cream shop. I continued with her until I left Wilmington. I sometimes wonder about these girls and whatever happened to them. I hope all good things, of course, but based on what I knew of them, I feel that may not be the case, unfortunately.

★ How to be an effective mentor

★ How to connect with troubled youth

★ How to be creative with my teaching skills

★ How to listen to my gut, to say no, and not get taken advantage of

★ How to admit when I am wrong because it happens to all of us!

# Ford Design

While I was working at Papa John's, the fire department, and mentoring, I ended up falling into another position. I was on the hunt for a new place to live and had been searching the papers (because this was the 90s, and the internet wasn't big yet). I happened across a guy named Sam and went to check out his place because it was in a decent neighborhood near campus and the fire department.

Sam and I hit it off right away, but I decided I couldn't live with him. I could feel that he was interested in me and that would make any living situation too uncomfortable for me. I ended up renting a house closer to the beach with a woman named Dorothy, but Sam and I became friends and went out occasionally.

One of his good friends, Greg, happened to own a marketing firm called Ford Design. One time while we were all out for drinks, Greg asked me if I would be interested in coming to work for his company. I had no experience in marketing, but I am a fast learner, so, of course, I said yes.

For the most part, I could make my own hours, which is something that I have always loved. I worked for him two to three days a week, around my school schedule. He had some big-time clients down in the

Wilmington area. And he and Sam were getting stretched too thin with the work load, so that is where I came into the picture. A lot of what I did was errand-running, answering phones, organizing the office, scheduling meetings, meeting clients for and/or with mockups, and sometimes giving my thoughts on particular projects.

During this time, I learned a lot about marketing, screen printing, embroidering, etching, ordering, and delivering goods. Most of my time seemed to be on the road. I wish I knew then what I know now because I would have written off all of those miles on taxes! Not only that, but I would have changed what I was eating to fuel myself during these long jaunts all over the area. I found that driving this long made me tired, so I would pick up candy and sodas from the convenience store to fuel me. Ah, the hindsight of an older and wiser person lamenting on the brilliant stupidity of her younger self! Even though there were things I could have done differently, at least I got to meet a lot of great people in the area during my stint with the company. They also hosted a lot of beach parties for the more well-to-do in the area, so I got to attend those under the guise of helping. Most of the time, that meant serving drinks or passing out marketing materials for whichever company we were marketing for. I got to dress up for these events, and they fed me, so I really couldn't argue. I want to say that what I learned the most was how to maximize my time and how to connect with a certain caliber of clientele. I would have stayed with them longer than a year, but I had grown tired of Wilmington and really needed a change. Therefore, I left the area and subsequently the job with Ford Design.

**14**

**What I Learned**

★ How the marketing world works

★ How things get screen-printed and embroidered

★ How to plan my driving routes so my time was most effectively spent

★ How to put together marketing packages

★ How to interact with higher caliber clients

★ How to organize a disorganized office to create organized chaos!

# Disney World

How in the world did I end up here, you may be asking? Well, that is a pretty simple, yet slightly interesting, story. As previously mentioned, I was at the point where I needed a change and longed to leave the Wilmington area. And it just so happened that Disney World had sent recruiters to campus, looking for fresh bodies to try the Disney World experience. A friend told me about the recruiters being present for a two-day time period, and I figured it couldn't hurt anything to go and talk to them.

I wish I could remember the recruiter's name I spoke with; she was very friendly and easy to connect with. I told her I was looking for a change and gave her a brief rundown of my work history. This is something they ask for so they have a better idea of where to place you, should you decide to accept a position with them for the six-month *paid* internship.

This is where my history with the fire department kind of screwed me. The recruiter was so excited by the fact that I was a female firefighter, she forgot everything else about my work history.

When I got my assignment a few weeks later, I found out I was assigned to Magic Kingdom in ODF (Outdoor Foods). This was really disappointing to me because I had specifically asked to be placed at Epcot in one of the lands in Food and Beverage. I called the recruiter and asked her why I was placed where I was and if it could be changed. After speaking for quite some time, and her pulling up her notes, she realized she *forgot* to put any of my other work history other than the fire department. And they had placed me in ODF in Magic Kingdom because that is where most of the lost children end up, and they needed strong people to keep them calm while security waited for the family to be found.

She told me they couldn't switch my assignment and apologized. I told her I had to think about it because I was so ticked. Eventually, I decided I would still take the opportunity because it would get me out of Wilmington and it was a job.

I left Wilmington in early August and headed to Florida for a new adventure. I had a close friend living in Savannah at the time, attending SCAD (Savannah College of Art and Design), so I stopped there along the way to break up the long trip.

When you join the Disney World internship program, part of the deal (at least back then) was that you had to live in their gated apartment housing, with other interns in the program. This gated community is called Vista Way, aka Vista Lay. Yep, that's a lovely nickname, isn't it? You may be asking why it would be nicknamed that. Well, that is simply because it was the number one place in the US, at the time, to get an STD. Nice, right?

The apartments were all either two- or three-bedroom, and each one had either four or six interns per apartment. I was assigned to a six-bedroom apartment, so I had five other female roommates. Now just try to digest this for a minute, if you will. A small three-bedroom apartment crammed with six college-aged, hormonal females. Does that sound like a good time to you? I can assure you it really wasn't all unicorns and rainbows.

I ended up having two "room" mates during my couple of months there because people leave the program regularly, unbeknownst to me. My first "room" mate left after a couple of weeks because she was homesick. I was sad to see her go because we got along pretty well, especially for having to share a room. After she left, I had the room to myself for a short period of time, which was a nice respite, since the other four girls were still in the house, and there was always some sort of drama going on.

On a side note, this is where I taught myself my current form of meditation. I needed to find a way to escape, besides running around the complex, which I did regularly, so I found books on meditation at the local library and adopted my own method.

When it came to work, I worked forty hours a week for Disney World. Since I was in ODF, I never knew which land in Magic Kingdom I would be placed in, day to day. Employees weren't allowed to drive onto the property, so we had to park in an employee lot and take a shuttle in. Magic Kingdom is full of underground tunnels, which is where all employees get their uniforms and eat lunch at the cafeteria.

I always liked walking into the tunnels because it felt so secretive. Costuming was another one of my favorite things because I knew, as soon as I saw which uniform they gave me, where I was for the day. Not only that, but once I was dressed, I got to pop up in different parts of the park through different hidden entrances. That part always felt pretty cool to me because I would continually stun park guests when I just showed up out of nowhere.

When I was in Florida, I spoke Spanish almost fluently. I knew some Spanish prior to living there, because I had taken it in school, but I have always done better with immersion. It helped that two of the five roommates were native Spanish speakers, albeit from different countries, so they had a hard time understanding each other. There was a third roommate who was from Texas and spoke Spanish, also, but this was yet another completely different dialect. This whole scenario was pretty hilarious to me! It also helped, though, that a lot of the guests we would run across in the park spoke Spanish. So I learned a lot during my time there, with respect to the language. I just wish I retained it.

I did end up rescuing more lost children than I can count, though. I have always been pretty good with children and calming them down, so this did end up being a good position for me. However, we were told we weren't supposed to be giving the lost children any of the ice cream, popcorn, or sodas while they were in our care. I was told this was due to the fact they couldn't ask the parents to pay for the goods once they were found. Most of the time, I abided by this procedure, but there were other times when I did not. This was particularly the case whenever I had children with me for over an hour or more. At that point, most of the time, they were really scared their families weren't going to come back for them. I still had to work whichever cart I had for the day, on top of keeping a really scared kid calm. So bring on the ice cream!

Overall, this was a good learning experience for me about what I didn't want to do with my life. The direct supervisors weren't very nice to us interns, and the pay was shit (hence internship!), so I ended up looking for a way out.

I had a hard time connecting with anyone during my time in Florida, and I never found a niche where I felt I fit in. A lot of times, if I had time off, I would take off in my convertible and just drive. I ended up all over Florida, completely alone.

This was a pretty lonely time for me. I had my reasons for fleeing Wilmington, and they encompass the darkest time in my life. So it probably wasn't beneficial for me to try to connect with anyone anyway in the state of mind I was in. Basically, I was severely depressed. It is the only time in my life I have been depressed, but this depression lasted for about two full years. I disconnected with most of the people I had known prior to the depression hitting and didn't really make any effort to connect during that two-year period.

This depression was also the driving force for me to leave Florida. I hadn't found what I was looking for, and it wasn't helping the situation. So, once again, I removed myself, like a thief in the night. I made a decision to leave and fled Florida within forty-eight hours of that decision.

**15**

**What I Learned**

★    How to differentiate various dialects in Spanish

★    How to live with five other girls in a small apartment and not kill one another

★    How to be more adaptable to different environments, depending on the day and the costume

★    How to keep scared children calm

★    How to effectively meditate

★    How to find my way around an alien environment, completely alone

# Tony Roma's

While I was working at Disney World, I decided I needed a second job to help sustain me. Not only was the pay crap at Disney, but I had too much time to kill, due to my depression and not wanting to create relationships with other people. Couple that with the fact that my brain was bored to death and numb, and I started looking for another source of entertainment and income. Enter Tony Roma's.

Now, at this point in time, I did eat meat, even though it wasn't much. I never liked ribs, so it's funny that I ended up waiting tables at a rib joint. But it was right down the street from Vista Lay, and they were willing to work around my Disney World schedule. It also cut down on my alone time and gave me something else to learn. So this was a win-win for me.

I can't say there was anything extremely memorable about this job. It was an easy waitressing position, except with ribs. The staff was the same as it is in pretty much every restaurant, just different faces and different names. They used a different POS system, so for me, that was probably the most exciting thing going on there. But it distracted me and put some more money in my pocket.

When I made the decision to leave Florida, I let them know I would work out my last two shifts on the schedule that week, but that I wouldn't be back because I was moving. They said they understood, but they were still sad to see me go because I was such a hard worker. Even to this day, I appreciate sentiments like that expressed to me.

**What I Learned**

16

★ How to serve meat when I don't eat it myself

★ How to deal with scheduling issues

# Dillard's

When I left Florida, I headed directly to Savannah, Georgia. My friend knew I needed to escape for a while, and even though I had mostly disconnected from her, also, she understood and offered me a soft place to land.

She was letting me stay with her rent-free at her tiny one-bedroom apartment off of Perry Street, in downtown Savannah. Besides the continual roaches and the tour bus that came by at random hours to talk to tourists about our building, I really liked the place.

I spent a lot of time working on my nature photography, and I even got to use some of the development studios at SCAD (Savannah College of Art and Design).

This was another place where I spent a lot of time alone, just wandering and stuck in my own head. I found Tybee Island one day, on a drive, and loved the place so much I returned regularly, just to walk alone on the quiet beach.

After spending a few weeks like this, I decided I needed to get a job to help pay the bills, as well as occupy my time. After going by quite a few restaurants down by our apartment, with no luck, I made my way out to the mall. I applied for a few different positions there and got accepted at Bath & Body Works. I told the hiring manager I would think about it, though, after she told me what the pay was, and that I'd get back to her the next day.

Luckily for me, Dillard's called later that day for an interview and hired me on the spot. They were a much better choice for me because not only did they offer me more money but I really have a hard time with the strong scents at Bath & Body Works.

I was put in the Home Department, which was great with me because I have always loved to cook and I'm really not a big fan of clothes. Selling them or wearing them!

I'm more of a free spirit and have never really cared much about clothing. I would much prefer to roam around naked—and do so frequently—in my own home and backyard. I am very comfortable in my own skin, and clothes just make me feel restricted, so they aren't on my high list of priorities. The only downside to this is that most other people in society don't approve, so I do my best to hide my natural preference from the outside world. But when in my own house (and backyard pool), when no children are around, it's free game to do what I want!

This job was extremely easy for me because it entailed restocking, setting up and breaking down displays, and, of course, selling products to customers. We didn't earn any commission on our sales, but our reviews and potential raises were based upon our sales.

Therefore, they had a weekly meeting with us, as a team, to discuss where our numbers were at and, if we hadn't met them yet, where we needed to be. I didn't have any problem meeting my numbers because I am good with people. It was also easy for me to convey what the purpose of these products was and the best ways to use them.

I enjoyed the job but not all of the female drama that ensued. I just really don't have the patience for that, which is probably why I've always had more male friends than female. They are simply less dramatic.

However, all good things must come to an end. I had been driving back to Raleigh regularly, and Dillard's needed people to work a regular schedule during the holidays. I had no problem with that, but after asking for a day off so I could drive up to Raleigh for Christmas, and then being denied, I decided I was done. I did come back and work the scheduled day, as well as the rest of the week, because I am responsible. But after that week, the end had come, and I left Savannah so I could go back to school in Wilmington.

**17**

**What I Learned**

★   How to merchandise for holiday sales

★   How to sell products I don't use or relate to

★   How to work in a highly dramatic environment

# Temp Agency Work

When I got back to Wilmington, I threw myself into school again, full force, just to try and get it wrapped up. I still didn't know what I really wanted to do or what my major should be, so I took it upon myself to find some more jobs to make money and occupy my time. I went back to the fire department, though, as one of them, of course, but was looking for something that paid more, also.

Enter the temp agency I heard about from a friend. I contacted Premier Staffing, and they brought me in for an interview and some tests. Now please keep in mind that this was before everybody had a laptop, so I had to do the computer-skills tests onsite.

I don't recall my exact WPM score, but I know it was high because I've always typed fairly rapidly and with accuracy. They were impressed with my computer knowledge and the fact that I was professional, so they started sending me out on gigs right away. These gigs paid anywhere from $8 - $10 per hour most of the time. This is *not* great money, but it was more than I was making at the fire department, and the work was steadier, so I was thrilled to have it.

I don't recall all of the odd jobs I did for the temp agency, but I do recall some of them. Most of the time, I was doing something very rote and mundane such as data entry. A few times, though, I got to do things with my hands instead. I really liked those jobs because it was something more physical. One of the gigs was for multiple days, and I was tagging and boxing up marketing products. This wasn't anything extremely exciting, but it was fun, especially since I'd spent some time in the marketing world already.

After doing this for a few months, I decided I wanted to find something that regularly made more money and might even have benefits, so I set out on my search.

**18**

**What I Learned**

★ How to work across multiple platforms for the same company

★ How to work quicker to procure more jobs

★ How to know when I'm underpaid for my skill set and find something else

# Sam's Club

A round this time, one of my ex-sorority sisters (this is a story for another book) had started working at Sam's Club, and she told me they were hiring. They were looking for college students for full-time positions and were offering benefits. They were also willing to work around school schedules, which was a bonus in my book.

She contacted her manager, to let him know I was interested, and I had an interview scheduled the very next day. This interview followed suit, as pretty much every other interview I have partaken in, in my many years in the work force. By this, I mean that it was short, sweet, and to the point. I met him, told him my background, and was hired in about ten minutes.

I was to be a front-end cashier and work forty hours a week, with benefits, and was starting the next week. No more temp work for me! The pay was only $10 per hour, but I had vacation/sick/holiday pay, health insurance, and a 401(k). I was pretty stoked about it. Plus, on top of it all, I got a store discount. I felt like I was winning the lottery. And it was so easy!

I actually really enjoyed this job because it was labor intensive, and

I got to have contact with the public and make human connections. My biggest issue in the work force has really been when I am forced to work behind a computer for many hours a day and have no human contact. As a naturally social person, interacting with other people is something I need in order to fully thrive.

I liked figuring out the registers and lugging large packages into customers' carts because it was like playing Tetris most of the time—a skill which I have fully honed throughout the years!

The other employees were nice to me, and a lot of them showed me the ropes in other departments. I was told that, if I wanted to start making more money, I would need to move up to another position such as working in a specific department. I never got to the point where I switched departments because yet another job came along that offered me more money, with the same flexibility and benefits. Who was I to say no to that? After only being at Sam's Club for about three months, I headed off to greener pastures, right down the street.

**19**

**What I Learned**

★     How to effectively use a box-cutter without cutting myself

★     How to sign up for a 401(k), and what that meant

★     How to solve issues with a cash register quickly in a fast-paced environment

★     How to use a bailer

★     How to stack products to maximize the use of the space, Tetris style

# Home Depot

The same friend who brought me into Sam's Club just happened to get plucked by Home Depot for more money not too long after I started at Sam's Club. She was the reason why I was only at Sam's for such a short period of time because she then plucked me to come work at Home Depot. While she worked in Outside Garden, they wanted me for Inside Garden.

They offered me $12 an hour, plus benefits, and didn't even interview me. I literally just walked in to meet the manager and sign paperwork. The reason why they put me in Inside Garden was twofold. The fact that I am horrible with plants and great with machines was the first reason. But the second reason was because it was hard to find females to work in Inside Garden, since most of them wanted to work with the plants.

I was the complete opposite and wanted nothing to do with them. I was much happier playing with lawnmowers and chainsaws all day. Yes, I know, I am basically a man in a woman's body. I've heard it before, and it will probably never change!

I loved the fact that, whenever somebody brought in a machine, I got to take a look at it first, to see if I could fix it. If the issue ended up being something beyond my level of expertise, and nobody else could figure it out, either, then we outsourced it.

One of my other favorite parts to this position was creating awesome end caps. End caps are the displays at the end of each aisle and/or sometimes at the front of the store. Each store would get graded on their end caps by the district managers, and I wanted ours to be the best. It probably helped that I have an interior designer for a mother, so I'm pretty good with creating things that are aesthetically pleasing and proportionate for the space.

On top of this, they wanted us all to engage in regular PK's (Product Knowledge) to enhance our knowledge of other departments. These were something I embarked upon with enthusiasm because I love to learn, and I really liked to be able to point customers in the right direction.

I became pretty well versed in electrical, plumbing, and lumber, as those ended up being my other favorite departments. Due to my love for those departments, I was given some latitude to build displays for the store, also.

After being back in Wilmington for nine months, I decided I had enough of the town and the school, so I left and moved back to Raleigh, temporarily. In order to do this, I had to request a transfer to a location in or near Raleigh. Once they granted it, they transferred me from the Wilmington store to the Cary store, and in Cary was where I built my first display house with a roof.

The roof took me a while to figure out because of the angles, but I finally got it, and it was absolutely fantastic! I put it near the cleaning supplies in Inside Garden and filled the top part with mops and push brooms, and the sides were filled with cleaning sprays. I named it the House of Glass, and I heard it stayed there for a few years after I left the company, and then some lucky employee took it home to keep.

The other area I worked in, at both locations, was inventory. We all had to help with the annual inventory, so I learned a lot about it on a more massive scale. But I began to try to keep better tabs on inventory, due to the fact I hated having to tell a customer that our system said we had two in stock, but we probably really had none. Nothing is more frustrating, in my mind!

I worked on keeping inventory in check in my department; I also started working on transfers. What I mean is I started to notice that customers would request certain things frequently, and we would always be short, while other products wouldn't move because we really didn't have a need for them in our area.

Therefore, I started searching other stores for these products and began playing the transfer game. If I needed a product and could find it at any other location in the country, I could contact them and ask for a transfer. It was up to their discretion, of course, so I came up with a system. I would make a list of what we needed and what we had a surplus of, and then find stores to make a trade with.

Whenever I found a store that had what I needed, I went down my list of surpluses to see what I could offer them in return, to entice them into making the transfer with me. It worked most of the time, and by doing this, I increased not only our revenue but the revenue of the stores I transferred with. Because of this, they started calling me the Transfer Queen. This was hilarious to me because it was simple math, but I was okay with it.

At this point, I was working the early morning shift, which I loved because it was either 5:00 a.m. – 2:00 p.m. or 6:00 a.m. – 3:00 p.m. However, I was also still cocktail waitressing at Crowley's until 2:00 a.m. a few days a week. After a while, the lack of sleep started to wear me down, and I began looking for another job in the building industry.

20

**What I Learned**

★   How to take inventory on a massive scale

★   How to fix small power equipment

★   How to perform basic plumbing fixes

★   How to perform basic electrical fixes

★   How to cut lumber properly

★   How to build a house, even if it is only a small display

★   How to build creative end caps to increase sales

★   How to transfer products between stores to maximize product by area

# Substitute Teacher

While I was working at Home Depot and Crowley's, I took on some other work. Crowley's was killing me with the late nights because I had to get up so early to be at Home Depot. So I cut my hours down at Crowley's and looked for supplemental work.

I found that, since I had experience mentoring children previously, and Wake County was in need of substitute teachers, I made a good fit for this position. So, I applied for this part-time job and got approved within a week. They had to perform a background check, obviously, but I could pick and choose which jobs I took. This way, I could work it around my HD schedule and still bring in some extra money.

They would call each night with jobs that came in that fit my criteria. I wasn't very picky about which jobs I took because I love a good challenge. I did find they had a tendency to put me in middle schools or in high school gym classes.

Working with the elementary school children was my favorite because they are at such a sweet age then and still full of wonder. They haven't started to go through the crazy hormonal changes of preadolescence, and they don't have the know-it-all attitude of the high schoolers.

But for one reason or another, I was pretty good at keeping the high school kids under control and getting them to do something in class that was educational. I had no problem doing anything I was supposed to be teaching in gym classes, so that may be why teachers started to request me for those positions.

All I know is that I enjoyed it, and it was easy to work two days a week at this job, when I wanted to, because it worked around my HD schedule nicely.

I did this job for a little over a year, until I left Home Depot and started at my next corporate job.

**21**

**What I Learned**

★ How to wrangle high school students

★ How to engage students with material I am unfamiliar with

★ How to fully maximize my time with multiple jobs

★ How difficult being a substitute teacher really is

★ How to *not* sleep and still function

# Selling Golf Club Passes

I can honestly tell you this job was my least favorite of any job I've had, to date. I'm really not sure how I even fell into this one, as it is entirely uncharacteristic of my job history, but I did.

At this time, jobs were advertised in the Classifieds section of the newspaper still and some—I mean very few—had started to advertise online. I found this one in the paper and figured why not. It seemed like it would be easy enough, even though I didn't really know much about the game of golf.

I called the number in the ad and was asked to come in for an interview the next day. Their "office" was located in a rundown office park and was furnished with basically nothing. It was pretty much an empty office space, with the exception of a couple of desks and chairs. This kind of took me off guard because it was unlike anything I had run across before.

My interview wasn't really even an interview but more along the lines of "you're hired." I started that day, and my job was to walk around to different business parks in the area and try to sell golf "memberships." These memberships consisted of a sheet of full-color tear-sheets that had different coupons for specific golf clubs in the state.

I absolutely hated this job and made basically nothing at it. It was a few days wasted out of my life, but I learned some valuable lessons about myself.

★    I *hate* cold-calling in person

★    I do not like selling crap

★    Don't get roped into some "easy-to-make" money because it never works out that way

# Selling Photography Sessions

This job was another strange one that just fell into my lap. I was walking in the mall one day and ran across a kiosk with a bunch of professional portraits displayed. The person manning the booth started talking to me about getting some professional photography sessions. While I was not interested in that, the person then inquired as to whether or not I was looking for a job.

Apparently, this representative thought I had a decent enough demeanor to be effective at selling photography sessions, even though I didn't want one myself. But I was actually looking for work, so I inquired as to what the job would entail, as well as to what the pay scale was.

I was told I would be needed in the office to follow up with leads and close the sale. Basically, the people manning the kiosk would bring in the paper leads from the mall and give them to us to get the appointments booked. The pay was to be minimum wage plus commission from every appointment we booked that resulted in a paid-for package.

This sounded easy enough to me. Plus, I have a pretty good phone voice and etiquette, to match. So this seemed like it would be a piece of cake.

Well, that's not really how it panned out. Big surprise there!

They did put me in their "makeshift" office, which was in an actual office building. But I shared a folding desk with a few other people.

They only wanted me in there for a block of three hours at a time, twice a week. So this was already not looking like much in the way of pay. But I was willing to give it a shot while I continued to look for other opportunities.

Let me just tell you that people can be really darn nasty sometimes. Even though these leads gave out their information to the kiosk rep, most of them were not thrilled to hear from me. I got yelled at quite a lot. And it wasn't that I wasn't being friendly, because I was.

After all, you catch more flies with honey than you do with vinegar. At least, that has always been one of my basic philosophies, and it didn't vary in this particular case.

It was very difficult to get anybody to commit to a photography session, even though they stated that they were interested. Not only that, but the photographer's pricing was a little bit cheaper than Glamour Shots (which was the big competitor to all photographers at this time). So this should have been a pretty easy sale.

But alas, it was not!

Unfortunately, I can't remember exactly how much I ended up making during my one-month stint, but it wasn't noteworthy. I believe I ended up getting a very minute commission from one sale, but that was it, besides the minimum wage. I was able to make more waiting tables. And I didn't get yelled at while I was doing that, so it made more sense to just keep that up instead.

**23**

**What I Learned**

★ Not all "easy" jobs are really that easy

★ Selling with a lead-base can still be really difficult

★ I greatly detest being on the phone all day

★ I could make much more at other jobs that I actually enjoyed

# Bell & Associates Interior Design

**B**ell and Associates happens to be my mother's company. As an interior designer, she is absolutely fantastic at her trade. She has not only designed some of the most fabulous concepts but has helped start different organizations within her interior design space. She is a go-getter and a force to be reckoned with in her field.

However, as fantastic of a designer as she is, she does not have the aptitude for accounting and organization. That is where I came into the picture. As her daughter, I grew up around her interior design world, so I have a good understanding of it. But I am also very much my father's daughter, in that I am pretty good with numbers and like accounting. I'm also a whiz at organization.

In fact, my brother, who I also do some work with (which will come up later in the book), tells me I am the Queen of creating organized chaos. I'm not sure if that is a compliment or not, but he says I can create organization out of chaos very easily. This is true about me. In fact, I take it as a challenge and look at chaos as a puzzle to be solved. So anything in the problem-solving space works well for me and my inherent personality.

Either way, my mother asked me to assist her with her company back in the late 90s, when I moved back to Raleigh, "temporarily." I've been helping her ever since, with a few random stints where I had full-time corporate work and could not.

She is the master at interior design, and I am her office manager. What does that mean, exactly? It means that I handle all of her books (we use QuickBooks), office organization, setting up new clients, ordering some products, dealing with manufacturers/vendors regarding said products, informing clients of ETA's, scheduling installs sometimes, social media, marketing, and other random things.

I actually really like working with my mom because we work very well together. I am a good person for her to bounce ideas off of because I have an eye, like she does. But I don't have the interior design background, so I don't necessarily understand every concept she is telling me about. I just know what works well together and what doesn't—the majority of the time, at least.

One of the great things about the design trade is that there is a huge market twice a year that just happens to take place in High Point, NC, about an hour and a half from us. High Point Market, which happens every spring and fall, is when designers and manufacturers release all of their new designs and the color of the year. I consider HPM to be very similar to the fashion industry and Fashion Week. Not only that, but Fashion Week has a direct bearing on the color of the year chosen for the industry worldwide, so it trickles down into every market, including HPM.

This market is huge, a lot of fun, good networking, and really exhausting. On the upside, all of the vendors/exhibitors there usually have a ton of free food to offer, so we don't go hungry. Although, a lot of it is candy and baked goods, which doesn't do me a whole lot of good. So we usually pack our own snacks and water, as well as comfortable shoes so we can last throughout the whole day.

When we go to HPM, we're almost always on the hunt for products for specific clients, as well as the new technologies and styles abound. This is another really good bonding experience for us and one that I greatly cherish. It lets me see more deeply into her world and what she loves about her chosen trade and how coveted she is for her expertise.

She is very good at design and customer relations but not as good at remembering to bill her clients. That is another place where I am highly proficient. I run through the books once a week to see where we're at and if anything is outstanding, and to make sure to get it taken care of. We bill our clients monthly, so at the beginning of every new month, I have to basically duct tape her to a chair, to go through all of the billings with me, to make sure we aren't missing something.

The system we have has only increased in efficiency the longer we've worked together. Ultimately, I've worked with her for almost twenty years now, off and on, and it has only strengthened our relationship.

**24**

★ Working with a parent can strengthen your relationship

★ Working with a parent can make it easier to see things from their perspective

★ I absolutely love creating organization out of chaos

★ I love numbers and spreadsheets

★ I love creating lasting relationships with vendors

★ I love learning new things about different industries and how they affect our everyday lives, unbeknownst to us most of the time

★ I love problem-solving

# BUILDING THE REST OF THE HOUSE

# Builder's First Source (Windows and Doors)

This was really the only job I ever found in a newspaper. Yes, those things did exist way back when, and it was one of the only ways you could find a job listing, unless it was by word of mouth.

While I was still at Home Depot, because I was tired of the micro-management style there, I started applying for any and all jobs I ran across in the building industry. I found that working at Home Depot taught me I really liked this industry, so it made sense for me to stick with something along those lines.

I don't remember how many paper applications (because that's what you had to send out back then, or hand deliver) I submitted, but it was a lot! When I saw the ad for Windows and Doors Coordinator at Builder's First Source, I thought it sounded perfect for me and my skill set. I remember driving up there to hand in my application and thinking it was way the hell out in the middle of nowhere!

I didn't hear anything from them for almost two weeks, and then I got a call that they wanted to interview me because I seemed qualified. This was the *only* company that actually called me from my resume submissions, which was pretty disheartening for someone who is as adaptable as I am.

Having such an unconventional job history wasn't actually working to my benefit, at this time in my life, or for most of it, really. Employers are usually looking for experience in one or two areas. When they run across somebody like me, they don't usually think, "Fantastic, this person is diverse and can adapt to any situation!" Instead, they are usually thinking more along the lines of, "This person has no idea what they want to do, and they have done too many different things. They are too flaky and possibly a flight risk, so we don't want to stick our necks out and give them a chance, just in case this job isn't a good fit."

Let me just tell you how frustrating that is from my perspective! While I realize, now, how much it can cost to bring on a new employee, which is why companies strive for retention, they oftentimes miss the mark on diversity and adaptability. Having both of these skills means the potential employee (in this case, me) can learn and handle just about any situation. That's the kind of employee everybody wants. Companies just weren't seeing it from this perspective, and some still don't, today, which is why I never got called back from a resume, with the exception of this one time.

However, the interview went splendidly well, and they hired me on the spot. Yay! They offered me $13 an hour to start, which was more than I was making at Home Depot—although not much more, but I wasn't arguing. That meant I didn't need to try to pick up any more of those horrible side gigs for a while. I also planned to quit Crowley's for good, which I did about two months after I started with BFS. That meant there was a short (very short) period of time where I only had one job. This is amazing, I know!

I really liked the staff I started this job with. Karen was the person who had my job prior to me, but then a new position opened up in which she would be working with me but was more senior. This was a really good fit for me because we got along exceptionally well, and she was a good teacher. To top it off, our boss was awesome! I still sporadically keep in contact with him and our old GM because they were such fantastic people to work with.

My job was to coordinate the window and door installs between our crews and homeowners. We manufactured some of the doors and windows at our on-site plant, but the others were shipped in via outside manufacturers. Most of the time, scheduling with homeowners was a fairly painless task. But every now and then, I would get somebody who was just a royal PITA and wanted to make everybody's life miserable. I went out of my way to do everything I could for them, in hopes it would turn their sour demeanor around. Sometimes, it worked because they just wanted to be heard. But other times, they were just inherently unhappy people that nobody could ever please. I can't do anything with that, so I just did my job the best I could and wrote them off as having bigger issues in life.

We were in the middle of transitioning over from handwritten everything to getting documents in the new computer system. Part of my job was also to assist with transferring old documents in my department over to digital, along with organizing the massive filing cabinets into some semblance of order. That was an undertaking, let me tell you!

One of the perks of this job for me was learning more about how windows and doors are installed. This was an area I was not as well versed in and found interesting, especially with regard to what order things needed to happen with new construction versus lived-in houses.

As another added bonus, I learned a lot about how windows and doors are manufactured, as well as the different types of both. All of these things were a great education for me, and I am still grateful for them, to this day.

My office was a pretty large one, and it had some beautiful sliding French doors at the entrance. I had an interior office, though, so the lack of windows was a feature I was not as fond of. My desk was huge so that it could accommodate the install crews in the morning, when I was doling out assignments and giving them the rundown for the day.

The crew I worked with was a group of really great, hard working guys, and I appreciated all they taught me and everything they did to get the job done right the first time. Honestly, I would have stayed with this crew in this position much longer, but life and the company had other plans for me.

**25**

**What I Learned**

| | |
|---|---|
| ★ | It is possible to get hired just on your resume alone |
| ★ | There is a lot more that goes into scheduling appointments with home-owners than I originally anticipated |
| ★ | Sometimes, employers do love to see a diverse background, so don't let anything stop you |
| ★ | Having a good attitude when dealing with homeowners, or customers of any kind, can really help most situations |
| ★ | I am good at organizing and find it therapeutic |
| ★ | The order in which a new house is generally built |
| ★ | There are many more types of doors than I could have ever imagined |

# Dog Rescuing/Rehab

It was around this time that I accidentally got into rescuing dogs. I have always had a love for animals, all animals. This translated into me becoming the unwitting rescuer of lost dogs and abandoned puppies.

Before I moved back to Raleigh, I had rescued my dog, Kacyn, from Pender County Animal Control. She was such a sad looking dog and so scared of everything that I just couldn't leave her there. I worked with her to get her used to people again, after being so horribly abused during the first part of her life. Since I was also on a pretty tight budget, and used to problem-solving, I learned how to give Kacyn her vaccines myself. The only vaccine that isn't available to the public is the Rabies vaccine, but every other one can be bought at a Farm Supply store, along with the syringes. So I got creative and figured out how to shoot her up myself.

Because of working with my dog, my penchant towards abused and abandoned animals only grew stronger. Therefore, when people started coming to me to ask if I could help with a stray puppy or an abandoned set of puppies, I willingly obliged.

The first puppies that found me, so to speak, was a litter that was left with their mother in an abandoned house out in the country. The owners apparently just left the mother and seven pups to fend for themselves. People really are heartless assholes sometimes.

I agreed to take them all in because I had a fenced-in backyard, and it was just Kacyn and I. As soon as I got those beautiful, helpless puppies, I worked on bathing all of them and assessing the health of each one. All of them appeared to be in good shape, minus some flea action. But I worked out a deal with my vet for her to take a look at them and make sure there wasn't anything else wrong with them. Amazingly, she agreed to do it at cost, since she knew I wasn't keeping them but was trying to make sure they were in good health before finding them permanent homes.

All of the puppies were in good shape, except for one who had worms, but we got him treated. I had to quarantine that little guy in a separate space until those nasty old worms were completely taken care of, which we made sure of.

I was able to find a good home for the mother within a week. The new owners brought her back a few times to see the pups while I was trying to find each of them the appropriate home. I honestly don't remember how long it took me to find homes for all of them, but I did. And I only charged the new owners the costs I had incurred because I wasn't trying to make money off of this little inadvertent venture.

The act of rescuing and rehabbing dogs lasted close to three years, off and on. I didn't advertise my services because I wasn't trying to make a business out of it, although, in hindsight, I probably could have. I just wanted to help with something I was good at and had a passion for.

The last set of puppies I ever had was six Dalmatian puppies, who did not have their spots yet. They were adorable! But at this time, I had a second dog (one of the puppies from the original batch listed above) Keoki, and I was pregnant with my first child. I realized I just couldn't do this anymore because it had become too time consuming, and I had too much going on in my personal life and my house to have a lot of puppies running around in different states of rehab. So I didn't take any more puppies after that batch. But it was great while it lasted, and I loved every minute of it!

**26**

**What I Learned**

★ Sometimes passion and skills lead to an inadvertent job

★ How to give vaccines to animals on the cheap

★ How to negotiate with a vet to get a better rate sometimes

★ How to find new homes for dogs

# Jillian's

**B**eing in the restaurant industry for so long, I felt like a fish out of water by not being in any restaurant setting for work, even though I loved my new big-girl job at BFS. While I really liked what I was doing at BFS (yes, you can imagine what we actually called it with an acronym like that), I missed being in the F&B (Food & Beverage) scene. Since I was working a so-called nine-to-five now, I would still have some extra time to pick up night shifts somewhere a few nights a week for extra cash. I was immediately drawn to checking out a few potential options in the slowly waking downtown area.

Jillian's just happened to have an outdoor sand volleyball court, along with four different sections of the interior that were completely different. I liked the idea of this because it meant I could move around to different locations and not get bored with the same old scene.

I went in and applied and was hired on the spot, as was typical in the F&B industry because it's hard to find good people. They hired me initially as a cocktail waitress for the arcade section and the bar/pool hall section. Both of which seemed like I would be a good fit for, and they were completely fine with my irregular hours and that I was only going to be part-time.

When I first started, the staff and management were all fairly cohesive, which made it a good working environment. The tips weren't nearly as good in the arcade section as in the bar/pool hall section, though. This was due to the fact that most of the patrons in the arcade section were families with smaller children. Not only did they not usually tip as well but the kids were always making giant messes! However, on the flip side, in the pool hall section, most of the patrons were couples, business men/women, and people in their twenties just having a good time. They drank more and ate more food, which equaled more tips for me, and they were usually less demanding. Why *wouldn't* I like that option more?

While this was a pretty easy side gig for me, I found that, even with more diversity, I got bored. Luckily for me, one of the other sections of Jillian's just happened to be a Hibachi grill, and they were short-staffed on the chef side. Due to that, I asked my manager one day if they would be willing to cross-train me there for the Hibachi chef position, and they seemed intrigued.

I started training to be a Hibachi chef (which is as much about the tricks as it is the cooking) and figured it out pretty well within my first few lessons. Once I was trained, instead of cocktail waitressing, I became one of their regular Hibachi chefs when I was available. For me, this was a pretty cool new skill, especially because it was rare to run across a female Hibachi chef. That made my tables fuller and my tips larger, so I couldn't complain. As a side note, this just happened to be where I met my first fiancé, who was a prep cook on the line for the Hibachi stations. But that is a longer story for another book.

I would have easily been content to keep on working for this company in the multitude of different positions and sections had they not decided to change the management. A lot of things in life come down to leadership and whether or not management has the skills or not, and such was the case here.

I worked at Jillian's for a little over a year as a side gig (or a side hustle as it is more currently well known to the general populace), but all good things must come to an end. One day, the manager that had been so great and easy to work with was no longer there, and a new person stepped in. This new manager had a completely different idea of how to manage, and it was not an effective plan.

He had the typical New Jersey management style I had run across before. If you don't know what that is, then you should definitely look it up! Basically, it is management ruled by fear. This management style attempts to put the fear of God into any and all employees so they know you are the gatekeeper of their survival and, therefore, will do whatever they tell you to do or take a verbal lashing if you don't. I'm sure this works for some of the more hardheaded folks out there, but I am not one of them. In fact, as a fairly intellectual individual, I find it offensive when somebody attempts to rule and control me with degrading language and verbal abuse. It takes everything in my power not to stand in front of them and laugh in their face. This style has *never* worked on me, and this time was no exception.

This new manager came in and held a meeting after a couple of weeks of watching and assessing the crew. Now, granted, there are a lot of hardheaded people in the F&B industry that sometimes need a firmer hand to get them to do anything to help the team, but that is not the majority. The majority of us just want to work and earn our tips and find a place that we fit into, just like everybody else. This man called a company meeting and informed all of us that, from that day forward, we would all be working a set schedule of his choosing, and that he would no longer tolerate part-time employees. We were also no longer going to be allowed to have our shift meal (which is fairly standard at most restaurants), and he was changing the dress code, even though we already had set uniforms.

I just looked at him like he had grown a third eye and hooves. After the meeting, I went up to have a discussion with him about said changes. He seemed to be on the defensive right off the bat, even though I approached him with my corporate, professional voice. The long and short of the conversation was that he wanted me to be full-time (I'm not sure what his plans were for the other few part-time folks, though) because he liked my work and my ethics, and he wanted me to be a stronger member of the team. While I understood that, and appreciated that he was a fan of my work ethic and my diversity, I already had a full-time job. This was a concept he was having a hard time grasping, as he wanted me to leave my full-time corporate job to wait tables full-time, and he became a bit belligerent about it. Just, NO!

In what world would this have even made a modicum of sense? None in my mind! He told me to think about it and get back to him on my next shift. This was not something I had to really think about, but I was going to miss the extra income, that was for sure.

On my next shift, I had a meeting with him about his request, and I denied him, of course. He was not happy about it because he had hoped the strong-arm tactics would work on me. He really didn't know me all that well if he thought that was going to work! Therefore, I gave him my two weeks' notice. At which point, he asked if we could schedule an exit interview on my last day, to which I said of course.

I worked out my last two weeks and was a little sad about it because

I liked what the place had been for me, the friends I'd made, and the new skill I picked up. But it simply just was what it was, and it was time to move on. So, on my last day, I had my exit interview with the new manager, who still tried to get me to change my mind. I wasn't budging on his request, and I told him that, if he kept up these tactics, he would run all of the good people out and be left with the shit. Everyone knows that, when you are left with the crap employees, your ship starts to sink pretty darn fast. I told him I didn't see this business being around much longer if he kept up the way he was planning to, because I had been around a while and had gotten pretty good at predicting this kind of thing. He didn't believe me, but he should have. That place was closed within two years, and it had gone to pot well prior to that, which is too bad because it was very diverse and entertaining in its heyday.

**27**

**What I Learned**

★ Cooking Hibachi is pretty fun and a technical skill that not everybody can do

★ I like learning new skills and cross-training in different departments

★ I never want to work in an arcade again

★ The bar always makes more money than the restaurant side

★ Good or bad management can really make or break a place

★ Change is constant, even if I am comfortable with the way things are

★ I am more than willing to walk away when somebody throws an ultimatum at me

# Builder's First Source
# (Panels and Trusses)

I didn't leave BFS, but I did get transferred to another location and another position. The worst part about all of it, besides really liking my job and crew, was that the location they moved me to was in another town nowhere near where I had just bought my first house. My boss knew ahead of time that our positions at that plant were going away and was working on creating jobs for us at the other location, unbeknownst to us. This was all happening while I was looking for my first house in downtown Raleigh and subsequently closed on it.

The current location I was working at was in Wake Forest, about twenty minutes or so north of my new house. The location they were moving me to was in Apex, which was closer to thirty minutes West/Northwest of me, and the traffic was worse. Needless to say, I wasn't thrilled.

But my boss fought for me and all of us to keep a position with the company, so I was grateful for that, along with the fact I purchased a house well below my means, on purpose.

My boss came to me about two weeks after I closed on my house, to tell me they were getting rid of our location and that he had worked out a deal for us all to move to another location, but I would have to switch positions to Panel Coordinator and work for a different boss. My choice was to take that or leave the company. Well, the decision seemed fairly obvious, so I took the position. We had a week left at our location before we had to move.

Once the move happened, I met my new boss and loved him as much as my previous boss. The perk was that both bosses actually worked together so they both could have a say in what was going on with the rest of us. However, we had a new GM, and he was *not* as friendly. In fact, he was kind of an arse, as was his direct assistant. They both managed with a New Jersey management style (here we go again!), which I don't take well to.

This style also does not allow for anyone to question decisions, and I naturally love to question everything. So, unfortunately, there was an immediate disconnect between us.

Both of my bosses tried to buffer me from their wrath (because they also weren't huge fans of women in the building industry, nor did they think they were intelligent enough to be there), but eventually it all came to a head.

Before that happened, though, I was there for about two years. I first worked with Bill who was the Panel Salesman. I was his Panel Coordinator, and I had to learn how to do takeoffs and read them in order to figure out the cost, per foot, for a turnkey quote. I also had to learn how to use the software provided and create spreadsheets (which I already knew how to do and love because I am a nerd). This was yet another new skill I never knew about and really thrived at. But after a while, I grew bored because I had mastered what I needed to know to help Bill effectively.

I started asking him to give me other things to do to stave off my boredom because I was getting to the point where I was dreading going into another monotonous day of work. He was able to help me out in this respect because this particular location was working on building a panel plant to begin manufacturing our own panels. What he needed from me was to go down to our Charlotte location and learn how to input all of the information into the panel software so that everything would automatically transfer over to our panel plant for production. We didn't have the software or the system in place yet, and this sounded like great fun to me, so I wholeheartedly agreed.

I went down to Charlotte for two days to train with their panel designer. At first, it was difficult for me to grasp, but after the second full day of training, I understood how it all worked and how to input the necessary information. I then brought back all of my newfound knowledge and was given the task of getting the system set up and taking over that position, along with my current one. This was all completely fine with me because I needed more to do to keep my mind busy. I also worked on training others how to do what I was doing, but for some reason, that didn't really take very well.

I guess what my son says is more correct than I'd like to believe: "Not everybody is you, Mom."

I came back to my home location and began setting up the panel system for the new plant, which was a challenge for me, but I liked that. In case you haven't noticed, there is an underlying theme here. This part was a lot of fun for me because it was a whole new world, and I was helping to set up a new system that nobody had seen or done yet. I love this kind of stuff!

Once I helped get the panel system up and running, they began to have me train another person on this particular facet of my job. The reason for this was to ensure that somebody else besides me knew how to perform this function (smart business sense there!) so I could go back to helping Bill more with the panel takeoffs.

However, the person they brought in for me to train didn't last very long. She just couldn't grasp the concept or how to operate the program. Unfortunately, she also happened to be a friend of mine, and that put a huge strain on our friendship. In fact, since the day she didn't show back up at work, we haven't spoken. I called her and left a ton of messages, asking if everything was okay and thinking she was really sick or dead somewhere. Her fiancé finally called me back much later that day and told me to stop calling her, that she wasn't coming back. That is the last I ever heard from either of them, and we were great friends, or so I thought.

That experience taught me to be much more careful, as to whom I recommend for a position because sometimes it not only affects my work life but my personal life, also.

Since she only lasted a few weeks, I was back on my own, working two different positions. This was fine with me, though, because it kept me busy and kept my brain active. After doing this for a few months, they finally found another person for me to train, and she was a much quicker study, in terms of the panel program. Once she was trained, she took over most of the panel system entering, and I was regaled to putting out fires or figuring out the more intricate issues. Both of which are things I happen to not only be good at but rather like.

Next, I got moved to a real office and out of the dreaded "Cube Land." I was so happy for that because I have always *hated* working in a cubicle. It makes me want to poke my eyeballs out with the nearest sharp-enough office supply. I realize that may sound drastic, but I hate it that much.

With my new office, I started getting more in depth with Bill and the panel takeoffs. By that, I mean he began to teach me more of the intricacies about how the turnkey system worked. Not only that, but he began to take me out on jobsites with him so we could check on the jobs and our crews. Some of the crews were in-house, and some of them were subs that we were using—this all depending on what function they were performing. But I can tell you that I got really good at speaking Spanish on the job, and this was hilarious to me. The reason why is that most of these crews never saw a woman on a job site, let alone one wearing a dress and heels, so they assumed I would have no idea what they were talking about. HA! One of my favorite things, in this type of situation, is to be underestimated. This is because it gives me a leg up. The element of surprise, if you will. Being underestimated before somebody knows me usually gives me an advantage because I get real insight into who they are and what they think I am capable of. But, once somebody knows me, for any length of time longer than five minutes, I get offended when they underestimate me.

Once Bill started taking me out on job sites, he began to give me the task of checking for OSHA safety violations from any of the crews. OSHA is the Safety and Health Administration, whose job it is to ensure the safety and healthfulness of all working conditions. In the building industry, they ensure that workers have the proper training and gear to perform their jobs safely. When I was checking for OSHA violations, I would have to go out to the jobsites and make sure that all crew members had on the proper safety gear, as well as had documentation filed with us for the safety classes they were supposed to take and pass prior to their specific job. Bill also had me go through everybody's paperwork and ensure that we had all of the legal documents and insurance information for each person on each crew. This is another thing I happen to be fond of because it is a combination of detective work and problem-solving. I thrive in that type of environment.

On top of that, a lot of the office people realized I was fairly tech savvy (having a father in computers since the early 70s will do that to a person) and started asking me to help them fix their computers. So now, people began calling my office for tech issues (both hardware and software) and sometimes even dropping off their computers in my office for help.

Although this was not what the company was paying me for, it was something that just fell into my lap, and I enjoyed it. Plus, as per my usual, I blew through my workload pretty fast most days, so I had extra time to kill. For me, this is the worst part about working a forty-hour-a-week job because I am usually done before everybody else and bored. That is how I keep getting roped into new things, which is great but just ends up adding to my workload for no extra compensation. This is another constant underlying pattern.

Even with all of those extra things on my plate, I began to get bored again. This is always what happens once I efficiently learn something new and assimilate it into my current organizational pattern. On the upside, the truss department had been looking at me for a little while because they realized I was good with programs and math. Both of these skills are required in order to design trusses. But I had resisted going back to "The Cave" to work for them because I was afraid I was going to get bored and that they wouldn't want me to diversify.

Therefore, I had resisted being open to learning this new skill up until this new point of boredom. But after time, I caved. I figured that it would just be a new skill to add to my tool belt and create more neural pathways. I realize I am a huge nerd with that line of thinking, but it has really come in handy in almost every aspect of my life.

When the manager came to me to ask me, again, if I would be willing to learn to design trusses this time, I said I would. This meant they were going to cross-train me while I was still working for Bill and that eventually they would try to bring me over to their side full-time. I wasn't sure how I felt about the ultimate grand plan, but I was excited to learn a new skill.

The first day they began training me was a Friday, and I was having a hell of a time figuring out roof planes in the AutoCAD system. AutoCAD is the system that we used—and many designers use the same system—to create and manipulate geometric shapes into a specific design. I knew what it was because I had seen it before, but I had never had the chance to play with it prior to this experience. It just wasn't making sense in my brain. So, I spent a lot of time that weekend driving around, looking at roof lines until it clicked in my head. By the time I went back to work on Monday morning, I understood what the program was doing with roof planes and how I needed to enter in the information.

Besides the assistant manager of the truss department, I was the only other female in a dark room full of men in cubicles. Do you remember me saying that I hated living in Cube Land? Well, this Cube Land was even worse because they kept the lights down so low it was like working in a cave, hence the nickname "The Cave."

My training didn't go on for very long before they began to let me fly solo on some of the easier projects. There was certainly a learning curve for me on this one because I was learning CAD at the same time as learning how to design roof and floor trusses. But I figured it out, for the most part, and it wasn't bad because it was a challenge. I was still doing some of my other work for Bill out in the light and that helped balance being trapped in the back, in the dark. But all good things must come to an end, and unfortunately, that was coming shortly.

After a while, the truss managers took me away from Bill entirely, and I spent the whole of my work-life existence in the dark. This was what I was afraid of to begin with, and rightfully so, because I know myself pretty darn well. I greatly detest only doing one thing, and I also really hate having everything I do being scrutinized. It got to the point where they would track me, and if I went out to talk to Bill or any of the other former people I had been working with, they would call me back into The Cave. I felt like a dog on a short leash, and I hated it!

Not only that, but the New-Jersey-management-style arse that I mentioned earlier just happened to have governing power over the truss department, and he really hated me. A woman with intellect, problem-solving skills, and logic was not in his wheelhouse, and I needed to be put in my place. Have I mentioned that I greatly dislike this management style, and the only thing that it does is piss me off?

Things came to a head with the arse, so much so that he was screaming at me in his office one day about what a waste I was and how he ruled my world and I had to do what he said, no matter what. Yeah, good luck with all of that!

I went to Bill right after that lovely tirade and told him I needed to come back to him full-time and that he needed to get me out of the truss department because it was simply too hostile for me, and I would be forced to quit. He wanted me back, also, because he had been drowning in work ever since the truss department stole me, so he went to bat to get me back. Seeing as I hadn't been with them exclusively for very long, it shouldn't have been too difficult, but that wasn't the case.

The arse wanted me gone so badly that he went to the GM before Bill could get to him and asked them to get rid of me altogether. This, in hindsight, was his plan all along because bullies don't like to have people around who don't comply with them. And I am not usually one for compliance with bullying techniques, obviously.

At the end of the day on a Friday, the two truss managers called me into their office and told me they were letting me go because I just didn't fit with their style. I thought maybe they were going to hand me back to Bill, which is what we both were fighting for, but they were irritated that I didn't end up liking their department as much as they did and that I didn't fit, so they wanted me gone altogether. So, I packed up my stuff and went to talk to Bill on my way out. He was so irritated that his face turned almost bright red. He told me not to worry because he was going to get me back, and he was irate at the truss managers for going behind his back because he had just told them, at lunch that day, that he wanted me back with him full-time. Oh, the joys of office politics!

At first, I was really ticked off because I did so many different things in this company for them. But ultimately, I was able to get unemployment for a couple of months, and I took some time off to look for a job that was a better fit for me. While Bill fought to get me back, everything came down to office politics and the fact that I didn't fit into the cog in the grander wheel that the company wanted me to. I was too diverse for them and that was an issue. In all reality, things work out the way they are supposed to, and if Bill had been successful in getting me back, I would have harbored major resentment towards certain people there, and it wouldn't have made for the best work environment. On top of that, I went on to bigger and better things!

**28**

**What I Learned**

★ How to figure a turnkey panel takeoff

★ What the proper steps are in the building process

★ The rules and regulations for OSHA violations

★ How to implement a production processing system for panels

★ How to fix a multitude of different issues with hard drives

★ What roof planes are

★ CAD

★ How to design roof and floor trusses

★ When people feel threatened intellectually, they lash out

★ Diversity is not always seen as a good thing

★ Office politics can be nasty stuff, and I have no patience for it

★ I really don't fit in corporate office culture

★ Being stuck in a cubicle is the bane of my existence in the working world

# Babysitting Again

Since I left Jillian's, I had some extra time to pick up another side gig. This time, I decided I would prefer to get out of the F&B industry and go back to doing something that was less stressful, something I really enjoyed. Babysitting.

I started scouring through paper ads and the few existing places online, seeing as this was prior to the existence of Craigslist. I found a few different potential babysitting gigs that would work with my current full-time work schedule at BFS. I also went through an agency, which I can no longer recall the name of, and they are no longer in existence, to my knowledge. This agency paired potential babysitters with families and did the background checks, which I thought was a great idea.

I went on a couple of interviews with families through this service. The family I ended up with had a two-year-old daughter, and they both worked full-time in the movie theater industry, so they had wacky hours. That worked out really well for me because I worked until around 3:00-ish in the afternoon during the week, and they usually ended up both working at night. Not only that, but they lived right down the street from my full-time gig, so it was meant to be.

When I first interviewed with the mother, I thought she really didn't like me because she seemed like a complete hard-ass. The father seemed to be much friendlier towards me. But I realized later that is just their personalities, and the mother and I actually became great friends.

I watched their daughter, Bella, three to four days a week, usually, and sometimes on the weekends. It all just depended on their schedules.

I would work with her on her letters and numbers, and we would play pretend. I made her dinner and gave her baths. We read stories, and I took her to the park down the street and to the neighborhood pool. She was such a wonderful little girl and had such spunk!

Bella kept me busy, and I really enjoyed spending time with her. Babysitting for me has always been an escape from Adultland because I get to just be a kid again. There isn't any adult drama or office politics. There is just laughter and play and, of course, sometimes whining, but that is the nature of the beast.

She is extremely memorable to me for many reasons. Being with her, I just got to be myself and laugh and have a good time. I got to be the natural teacher that I am and be silly. Bella helped me remember to breathe and that life didn't have to be so serious and stressful all of the time.

On top of it all, Bella is memorable to me because she almost died when she was five. She caught the flu that was going around right after Thanksgiving, and it just wouldn't go away. Not only that, but it kept getting worse, and they had to rush her to the ER. Her body had started to shut down, and she ended up in a medically induced coma, to hopefully save her life. She was in that coma for at least two weeks. I went to the hospital to see her a couple of times, and it was so difficult to see her that way. She was so small and had so many tubes sticking out of her.

I'm not a religious person, but I am spiritual. So while I didn't pray, per say, I did put all of my energy out into the universe, in hopes she would make it through this.

As a twist, her parents had actually separated a few months prior to this happening. Their relationship was strained, but they were still communicating and hoping to find a way to save the marriage. Then Bella got sick, and they spent all of their time in the hospital with her, praying she would make it through.

Bella eventually began to heal and was able to go home after Christmas—right before the New Year. They celebrated Christmas late, but they got to celebrate, none the less. Not only that, but her parents went to marriage counseling and got back together not too long after she came home. So, while Bella getting sick and almost dying was very difficult for everyone, it ended up being a happy ending for all. Please keep in mind they were very lucky this incident brought them so close together and made them realize how much they still loved each other and wanted to make it work. This isn't always the case, and I know about that first hand, as I got divorced when my children were small. As much as we wanted to make it work to keep the family together, we just couldn't get on the same page, and it ended up turning into a pretty nasty divorce—in the beginning, at least. Many years later, it was the best decision for our family. Even if it wasn't the ideal situation.

After she came home from the hospital, they enrolled her in Tai Kwon Do so she could become stronger. This practice really helped her heal, and she ended up becoming a very strong competitor.

I baby sat her for years after that, and then ended up watching her younger brother, Nicco, who just happens to be my godson.

That is how close the mother and I became. They attended my

wedding and both of my baby showers. Our sons are six months apart in age and were pretty close when they were younger.

But as time marched on, so did our relationship. That is a part of the story you will hear later in the book.

**29**

**What I Learned**

★    To remember that life doesn't have to be so stressful

★    Laughing and playing can be part of adulthood

★    Beautiful things can come out of near tragedies

★    I love to teach

★    People I may not hit it off with at first may actually turn into great friends of mine

# Grocery Delivery

During this same time period, and through which the same agency I found Bella's parents, I ran across another couple I hit it off with. They also happened to live a few neighborhoods down from where Bella's family lived. This family had a slightly different request than just babysitting, though.

The mother and I had a few phone conversations prior to me going over to meet them in person. They had an eighteen-month-old daughter, Jenna, for which they were seeking a caregiver a few hours a week, in the afternoon. But that wasn't really the main need they had at the time. Jenna's mother was still healing from her birth and had issues lifting and bending, so she needed some help with the laundry, washing and putting away dishes, and grocery shopping.

I had absolutely no issues with this request because I did all of those things for myself, anyway, and was pretty efficient at it. That can be attributed to my organized Type A personality.

The deal was that she would email me a grocery list for Whole Foods on Tuesday night or early Wednesday morning. I would go grocery shopping for her (and do some of mine while I was there) and then go to her house and unload all of the groceries.

I would also wash all of the dishes and put away any dishes that had been run through the dishwasher, as well as unload the dryer and fold all of the laundry. Then I would make Jenna dinner, and we would work on numbers or letters or just play. I usually gave her a bath after that and helped her brush her teeth. We would play for a little while longer, and then one of her parents would come in and pay me, and I would go home.

There were also some other times when they would ask me if I could just babysit so they could go out to dinner, or something along those lines. I loved every aspect of working for this family. I got to watch Jenna grow, and I learned a lot about Japanese cuisine—so many foods I had never heard of. It expanded my culinary palette and, for that, I am grateful.

I got along with both parents very well, even when they decided to get divorced. I didn't see Jenna's father too much after that because he moved to a different house, but whenever I did see him, we spoke like we always had.

Right before they ended up getting divorced, I got married, and they both attended my wedding. About six months later, my son, Reese, was born, which they were perfectly fine with me bringing to the weekly visit with Jenna. But once I had Reese, it became more difficult for Jenna because she wanted my full attention, and that was hard with a newborn. It became easier as he got older because Jenna would include him in our play. But she still wanted more of my attention, which was difficult sometimes. It became much harder once I had Presley because Presley is much clingier to me than Reese ever was.

Jenna and Presley had a continual battle over who would get my attention. I continued watching Jenna until Presley was two years old.

By that time, I had just started going through my divorce, and Jenna told her mother she didn't like me coming over with my kids anymore because I couldn't spend time with her alone when they were with me.

I was sad to see this relationship end, but it was time, as Jenna was eight years old by this point. I still keep up with her mother, and I've seen Jenna play in concerts a few times throughout the years. She has turned out to be a beautiful young woman, and I am so grateful I got to spend that time with her when she was young.

**30**

**What I Learned**

★ How to grocery shop with an infant

★ How to multitask household chores with a toddler

★ That balancing attention between children can be nearly impossible at times

★ Japanese cuisine and traditions are much more interesting to me than traditional SAD (Standard American Diet)

★ Being part of a child's formative years is something I greatly enjoy

# Special Programs
# Teacher Assistant

I've always loved substitute teaching and, really, just teaching, in general. Because of that love, I decided to start looking for jobs as a teacher or a TA (Teacher Assistant) within the county. It didn't really matter to me what I was teaching because I am adaptable, so I applied for everything I qualified for.

Ultimately, I was pretty sure that I wanted to work a year-round schedule because that would give me three weeks off every nine weeks. The way the year-round schedule works here, in North Carolina, is that students are in school for nine weeks and then get a three-week break. They go back to school again for nine more weeks and then get another three-week break. This cycle happens four times in a school year with a one-week break the week of Fourth of July to change grades. This seemed like an ideal schedule for me to work on my house, go on mini-breaks, or work some side gigs. But I also wanted to be fairly close to my house, since I lived in the downtown area.

In reality, I ended up getting two job offers and was torn. They were both for middle school, which I wasn't as thrilled about. For those of you who haven't ever had a middle schooler, or worked with them, they can be a real challenge sometimes!

The real deal was that they were both good schools, but the one close to my house was a magnet school that operated on a traditional school calendar. That meant I would have the summer off but nothing really during the school year. However, it was close enough to my house that I could potentially ride my bike to and from school most of the time. This was what I was hoping for!

The job for both schools was as a TA for Special Programs, so that didn't end up being a determining factor. But the other school, which was much further away, operated on a year-round calendar. So I was stuck in a dilemma. Should I choose the closer magnet school with the not-so-ideal schedule or the school further away that was not a magnet school with the schedule I desired?

I had two days to make a decision, and I eventually chose the school further away, with the year-round schedule. I don't really have any regrets with this decision, but I do wonder what would have happened if I had taken the other job because it was so close. I did end up really hating the drive to and from school every day, since I know I could have been riding my bike to the other school instead.

Ultimately, the Special Programs teacher I worked with was phenomenal! Ms. James had five children and was going back to school to get her master's degree so they could bump her up to the next pay grade on the state pay scale.

I had never finished my undergraduate degree, so Ms. James was integral in pushing me to finish it. She was pursuing her master's through the University of North Carolina at Greensboro. Her program, she said, was "almost completely online." She did have to go there to meet with a group once a month, in person, for one of her classes, but that was it.

She talked to me about the program and told me I really needed to consider finishing my degree if I wanted to become a full-fledged teacher. She admired my skill and my patience, as well as my ability to catch on quickly. But by not having a degree, I was holding myself back. So I took a look at the college and decided to enroll in the Liberal Arts program.

I have Ms. James to thank for persuading me to finish my degree, and even for introducing me to the program I enrolled in. It was a really great fit for me; I was able to get my studies done after work and also get some done at work during downtime. So I can't thank her enough!

With regard to the work aspect, I really enjoyed the job. I loved being able to create my own reading programs and science experiments for the kids. The kids we handled either had emotional or developmental delays. Basically, there were a few children that were on the autistic spectrum, but the rest of them were what people refer to as "troubled." This means they were the ones causing trouble regularly for all of the other children and teachers, and they needed to be removed and placed in a separate classroom.

We did have to create IEP (Individualized Education Plan) for each child, so this was a new skill for me. These were very in-depth and could be changed throughout the year, as need be, in the child's best interest. However, every year we had to have an IEP meeting with each child's parents, to go over what was designated and ensure there wasn't anything we were missing. This could get tricky sometimes because, more often than not, the parents of the "troubled" children didn't respond to our requests for meetings, they wouldn't show up for the meeting, or they were hostile or didn't care during the meeting. I found this to be a regular challenge and probably one of the factors that added to the children's "troubled" status. When there is not strong parental support and/or involvement, children seem to do worse in a school environment. At least, this was the pattern I saw regularly, and it made me pretty sad to see.

Luckily, though, the classroom we worked in was ours and could be a safe space for all of our students. Therefore, we got to create our own programs based on the needs and varying levels of the students.

Sometimes, students that were performing well would get to be reintegrated with the rest of the student body for a class or two, to see how they performed. When this occurred, we would have to walk them to the regular classroom and then pick them up at the end of class. This was one of the reasons why there needed to be two of us at all times. The other teacher would need to stay in the classroom with the students that were not being integrated.

There are two students, Drake and Spencer, that I remember vividly, even though it has been many years now. Drake held a special place in both of our hearts because he was such a sweet soul. He was the first child I ever worked with that had Asperger's, so it was a new experience for me. He was highly intelligent, but due to his Asperger's, he just didn't understand how to fit in with his peers. Although he tried a lot of times, he just didn't understand the general social nuances. Not only that, but he has typical Asperger's behavior, in that, if there was a subject we were covering that he loved, he was all in and was a voracious learner. But if it was a subject he couldn't care less about, he struggled mightily because it didn't translate properly in his brain.

Spencer, on the other hand, was one of the "troubled" children. He was sixteen years old and in seventh grade. In case it has been a while since you have been in middle school, that is an extremely advanced age for a seventh grader. This was due to the fact that he continually failed grades because of getting suspended and/or expelled. In reality, he was a pretty intelligent kid, but he simply did not apply himself. I blame his home situation, or lack thereof, because his parents weren't around, and he was being raised by a family member that really just couldn't take care of him. So he was left to his own devices in a less than stellar neighborhood, and with that, came falling into the wrong crowd. Both Ms. James and I worked with him a lot to try to help him with his perception and his outlook on life because we didn't want to see him end up in jail or dead before the age of twenty.

I do remember my last straw with him happened during EOG's (End of Grade Testing). I had to sit in the room with him while he took one of the tests, and he kept trying to talk to me, which is not allowed during these tests. I warned him that, if he kept trying to talk, I would have to take the test away from him, and he would have to retake it another day. Eventually, I had to take the test away from him because he was choosing not to heed my warning. This angered him to the point that he jumped up (and he was over 6' tall and well built, whereas I am 5'4") and started threatening to kill me. We were circling the round table we had been sitting at while he was yelling at me with veins popping out of his neck. I got close enough to the door leading back out into our classroom (because we were testing in the kitchen in between the two Special Programs rooms), ran out the door, and locked it from the outside. Ms. James was testing some other students in our classroom and asked me what was going on. I relayed the incident and told her to call the resource officer, to come and get Spencer until he could calm down.

I generally don't like my life being threatened, especially by a sixteen-year-old, over a test. So this incident really affected me. I went home that night and really thought about what I was doing and if it was what I really wanted to be doing. Not only that but was the money (and that is a joke!) really worth being threatened by a potential gang member?

When Spencer came back to school, he apologized to me, told me he still loved me (because that was his way), and gave me a hug. But from that point on, it was never the same with me because I remained extra cautious of him and his mood swings.

It was at this point that I began thinking about going back into the building industry. Not only was the money better but people weren't going to threaten my life regularly, so it was appealing. A good friend of mine from the BFS days had begun working for a building wholesaler, and she started to inquire as to whether or not I might be interested in coming to work there with her. This began my exit from my short stint as a TA in the education system.

To this day, though, I still think about Ms. James, Drake, and Spencer and wonder what ever happened to them. I did hear, through the grapevine, that Spencer ended up in jail not too many years after I left, but after that, I don't know what happened to him. Overall, I really enjoyed my time in Special Programs, and I learned a lot about the school system and how it operates, or lack thereof. In my opinion, there are just too many politics involved in the educational system which is one of the main reasons why it just isn't serving its purpose well.

31

What I Learned

★   How the school system operates

★   How to create my own reading and science programs

★   How to handle children with varying degrees of disabilities

★   How to create an IEP

★   Sometimes, parents are the contributing factor to a child's behavioral issues

★   That as much as I am a natural teacher, teaching in the school system is simply not for me

★   The pay is not worth the politics and the headaches, most of the time

# Event One Staffing

On top of being the full-time teacher for Special Programs, going to school to work on her master's degree, and raising five kids, Ms. James also moonlighted working security for a company called Event One Staffing. She had told me about this gig a few times, and it seemed right up my alley, so I asked her if she could introduce me so that maybe I could get on with them, also. She was more than happy to, which is just one more thing I am grateful for.

I had a phone interview with the owner of the company, and he hired me on the spot to work security at local events. This company ran security for Walnut Creek, NC State sports, and the arena where the Hurricanes play. I'm sure they probably service more areas now, but even with just those venues, they were pretty darn busy.

It was really easy to pick up side shifts with them, and I ended up usually working one or two shifts a week, on top of my TA job. Most of the gigs I worked were at Walnut Creek Amphitheater because it was a few miles down the road from my house, and I could ride my bike, which was my preference. If I recall correctly, they paid $10 an hour, which wasn't much, but it was better than nothing, and it was easy.

Plus, I got to incorporate my exercise for the day by riding my bike there and walking while I was running security circuits.

This job didn't require a whole lot of brainpower from me at all; it was almost entirely physical. Usually, at the beginning of the shift, they would tell us where we were stationed and when our planned break was to be. I got stationed usually out in the lawn or the perimeter where the vendors were, which was my preference because I got to do more walking and people watching. Let me just tell you, people are freaking weird!

One of the most interesting things I ran across, which began to happen more and more, was during a Phish concert. I came across a couple having sex on the other side of the lawn area, on the hill. Not only that, but they were high as kites, also, which was funny to me because I was completely sober. I told them they needed to put their clothes back on and go back to their seats, or I would have to remove them from the venue. They then proceeded to ask me if I wanted to join them and if I had a joint. HAHAHAHAHA!

After that, I ran across many more couples attempting to have sex out in the open, but it wasn't something that happened at every show. Certain shows just bring out certain types of people. For me, that made it interesting because I never knew what I was going to get.

A few times, they would throw me on the security line detail, and I would have to check people's bags, blankets, chairs, etc. on their way in. This was my least favorite detail, especially depending upon which concert I was working because people can get crazy. The one incident that sticks out in my mind was when I was working this detail while eight months pregnant with my son. The crowd was getting unruly because they wanted to get into the venue, and they started pushing each other. One man ended up pushing me, and I almost fell backwards, but I saved myself using the edge of the table. I was pretty darn ticked off. I told him to settle down and that, if he touched me again, he would not be allowed into the venue. Seriously, what is wrong with people sometimes?

After that, I stopped working events at Walnut Creek and did more work at the arena and the NC State football stadium because the crowds were a little less nuts. I continued to work for this company until my son was a little over the age of one. I liked it because it brought in extra cash, and I got to see some shows and sporting events basically for free. I would have continued to work for them, but life started to get a bit too hectic in our house, so I gave it up.

**32**

**What I Learned**

★     How to control an unruly crowd

★     People do really weird things at concerts they would never otherwise do

★     Side gigs can be a lot of fun and give me good exercise at the same time

★     I like listening to free concerts while I work

# Diamond Hill Plywood

If you will recall in the section about my being a TA, at the end, I mentioned that I started entertaining the idea of going back into the building industry. Well, I ended up doing just that because I was wooed by my former colleague's current employer, Diamond Hill Plywood.

Not only was the money better but they were only a few miles away from my house, so I could ride my bike to work a few days a week. This was a huge bonus for me! Although, I will tell you that this area was not very biker friendly on main roads and still really isn't today, so it was risky. But I always wear a helmet, and since I went into work earlier and could take side roads through neighborhoods for most of the commute, it worked out pretty well.

While the ride was nice, when I could work it in, the money was even better. Now don't get me wrong, it wasn't great, but it wasn't a teaching salary, either. I did have to go back to working 8:00 a.m. – 5:00 p.m., though, which has never been my favorite schedule.

There were only five of us in the office, and one of those was the branch manager, Richard. Chad was the guy who had been there forever and handled Purchasing. He is actually who I learned about commodities from, and I will be forever grateful to the little bit of knowledge he imparted upon me. Kaitlyn was in charge of Accounting, and she stayed in her office most of the time. That left Kim and I on the floor as the inside sales reps for our outside sales guys and any distributors that just happened to walk in.

When I worked at BFS, I was in a completely different part of the building industry than when I went to Diamond Hill. This part of the industry had to do with wholesaling building products to retailers such as Home Depot, Lowes, BFS, Stock, ABC, etc. Anything a contractor or a layperson off the street bought from them, they got from somebody like us first. We were basically middle men, which was an interesting concept for me. At the time, I didn't really know what a wholesaler was, but I quickly learned.

One of my favorite parts of this job was getting to do training with different vendors about their products. I think I was more excited about this than the other people in the office were, probably because of my deep thirst for knowledge. Well, that and the fact that I have always loved to build things, especially if I can make them more sustainable. So this was a great aspect of this job for me because I got to learn a plethora of information about new building products, some of which I had never heard of before.

I also got to learn more about all of the local distributors and what each of them sold. I loved the negotiating process, also, between myself and some of my distributors. Of course, there were favorites, so I would give them a better deal. But that is the name of the game with wholesaling. It's all about creating relationships. This is a skill I used very well in a later position and have utilized frequently since.

One of the biggest perks was getting an employee discount. This meant I could buy products from us to use on my house projects at a fraction of what I would normally be purchasing them for at a retailer. Why, yes, please!

During this time, I worked on gutting my kitchen and building a laundry room in my house, so this little perk came in handy.

However, unfortunately, my position at the company didn't quite last a year. Although I really liked working for them, I got bored easily. This is primarily due to the fact that I greatly detest being trapped inside and strapped to a chair, waiting for the phone to ring. And that was the bulk of the job. This goes against my nature wholeheartedly because I like to move.

I created other little projects for myself such as reorganizing the office and the filing cabinets. But even that didn't take up a huge amount of time. Since I had decided to go back to school and finish my degree, it actually worked out pretty well because I could do some of my online schoolwork during downtimes. This became a win-win for me.

While I was with them, I found out I was pregnant with my first child, my son, Reese. The original plan was to go back to work after he was born because we didn't know how we were going to make it work otherwise. At the time, I brought home more money than my ex-husband did. That meant we would be cutting our income by over half if I didn't go back.

But (and here is the *but*) after my son was born, I just couldn't do it. I couldn't fathom the idea of paying somebody else to raise him while I brought in money. On top of that, what I brought in wasn't extraordinarily more than what it would cost us to pay a nanny, the extra food for lunches, and extra transportation costs.

So when I was close to the end of my maternity leave, I went into the office to talk to Richard about staying on part-time or working from home. He wanted me to come back full-time, but I told him I just couldn't do it. He wasn't very happy about that, and he denied my request to work part-time instead. So this is where the story of my days at Diamond Hill ends. I left the building industry to stay home with my infant son. Or so I thought.

**33**

**What I Learned**

| | |
|---|---|
| ★ | The price of commodities controls a lot more in our market than I was ever aware of |
| ★ | How to negotiate with vendors/distributors effectively |
| ★ | Creating a personal relationship in business can really help get things done |
| ★ | I bore easily and detest being trapped in an office |
| ★ | Sometimes, family is simply much more important than a job |

# House Cleaning

Right before I gave birth to my son, my parents began asking me if I would be willing to clean their house a couple of times a month for extra cash. Since we were still trying to decide what we were going to do as to whether or not I was returning to work full-time, or at all, I agreed.

When I was thirty-nine weeks pregnant, I started cleaning their house. I have to say it was difficult for me the first few times because I was so hugely pregnant and had just given birth for the first time. On top of that, they have three floors in their near 5000-square-foot house, which was great when there were five of us living there, but since all of the kids are gone, many rooms weren't used regularly.

The first time, she walked me through how she liked for things to be cleaned and which products she used. Although, throughout the years, we changed some of those products to more natural, less toxic cleaners. One thing I did realize was that we have very different ways of cleaning, which took some getting used to for me. But even though she liked things to be done a different way than I was used to, I did learn there is always more than one correct way to do things. As a side note, I also learned that cleaning hardwood floors with vinegar and water is much safer than the more widely used hardwood cleaning products and extends the longevity of the hardwoods. That was a bonus lesson because that is how I have cleaned my hardwood floors ever since, and they look immaculate!

The order in which I worked was pretty methodical and usually took me about three to four hours to clean (depending on if I ended up talking to either of my parents while I was working or not).

Here is how the house cleaning went down:

1. Dust everything with a dusting rag, including all stair rails and ledges (I would irregularly add in dusting of the silk plants when needed).

2. Clean the bathrooms, starting with putting toilet cleaner in all of the toilets. Then systematically go around and clean all of the sinks, countertops, and showers/bathtubs, followed by the toilet in each bathroom.

3. Clean all of the mirrors and glass-top tables with window spray.

4. Swiffer the first floor.

5. Clean the kitchen countertops with granite cleaner.

6. Vacuum the whole house, starting with the first floor and working my way up (this includes the stairs, which was the hardest part whenever I was pregnant).

7. Mop the bottom floor and all of the bathrooms.

While it may not sound like a lot, please remember the size of the house. When I first started cleaning their house, they would pay me $100 each time. This was very helpful to me because it was money I could use for groceries and incidentals. It really helped out a tremendous amount later on when I got divorced and had no money because I really couldn't even afford groceries for myself and the kids.

On top of that, I got to spend extra time with my parents, and my mom would spoil the kids when they came with me. They loved that because they got treats at her house and sometimes she would take them out to the park or something else along those lines.

They were really doing me more of a favor than I was doing them, but with me cleaning their house, they had more time to focus on work. This was a really good lesson for me about working well with family, but it also translated well to the rest of my work-life and creating good relationships.

By this, I mean that learning what employers like, and the systems they prefer, is important to a good working relationship. The same can be said for doing things you don't like, but doing them well. Employers will show you more respect, and sometimes give you the better jobs, if you show you can efficiently and effectively do the stuff you don't like. A good example of this would be when I was working at Eddie Romanelli's, and I jumped into the dish pit multiple times, even though I hated it and it was disgusting. Because I willingly did that, and did it well, they began to give me better sections during my shifts, which translated into making more money, and I was okay with that.

Even though I have always been pretty good about going above and beyond, cleaning my parents' house taught me more about humility. They don't give anything for free, and I don't expect it. I think this has a lot to do with why I am the way I am, not just in my work-life but my personal life, as well. Nothing in life is free, but if you are willing to do something you might not otherwise entertain, it may hold even more benefits than you initially thought.

Did I like cleaning their house? Not really, but it was a good deal for all of us. And on top of that, other people started asking me if I would clean their house, also. But I never took anybody up on it because they couldn't offer me as sweet of a deal as my parents did.

★ Sometimes, jobs come unexpectedly

★ Just how long it takes to clean a big house (which made me more and more grateful for my much smaller house!)

★ There is always more than one way to skin a cat

★ Cleaning hardwood floors with vinegar and water is fantastic for the floors!

★ Working with family can be a very good arrangement

★ Nothing in life is free

# TriE Medical

Speaking of family, this job was another unexpected position with family. My father, to be precise. He has always been into computers, and we always had a multitude of them, and some of their associated parts, lying around the house. Not only was he a computer guy, but he was also a natural born entrepreneur. In fact, all of us either were at some point or still are. He owned a small business when we moved to North Carolina, but then ended up working for another company out of Israel called Angiosonics.

You may recall, but I worked with them when I was a teenager, and that was my father's doing. Well, it just so happened that two of the other engineers he worked with at Angiosonics became interested in creating a new company with him, so they did. And TriE Medical, Inc was born.

This company was a device prototype design and development firm. But they were only dealing with devices in the medical industry, since that is the area they had been working in for some time now.

The first year or so was tough, and one of the partners ended up leaving the company and moving to another state, so that left my father and one other partner, William. Ultimately, this is probably where the main issues stemmed from because it is hard for any executive decision to be made, in the case of a dispute, if there are only two 50% votes.

After I had Reese and became a stay-at-home mother, I became bored rather quickly. Not only was I bored, but the huge cut in pay was causing some major strain on me, especially since I was the accountant in the family. My dad was looking for some help getting things set up in the office and asked if I might be interested in helping out one day a week. A friend of mine said she could watch Reese (although after only a few weeks of that, my mom ended up taking over and loved her time with him) so that I could go into the office.

Originally, what they needed me to do was to go through all of our old documents from the Angiosonics days and change them to make them applicable to the new company for policies and procedures. This was something I was good at because I wrote some of the documents from Angiosonics, or had a hand in writing. A lot of them, though, I didn't have anything to do with the first time around. This meant I had to make major changes to the documents (as well as the headers and footers, of course) to make them applicable, or I trashed them altogether because they didn't fit with our new business model.

While I was working on this, they also had me set up all of the HR policies and procedures and the protocols for how we were going to handle employees. At the time I came aboard, we had four other people on our staff. William's daughter, Elizabeth, started working with us on the marketing side, Chad was running our machine shop, Doug was our hardware engineer, and Richard was our mechanical engineer. The three men were all with us during the Angiosonics days, also, so we had a history of working together.

Since my father was the VP of Finance, he had me working on the books with him. I handled all of the regular transactions, including purchasing, accounts payable, and accounts receivable. He handled the taxes because that was something he preferred to keep, which was just fine with me.

The other thing they had me start working on was creating an inventory system from the hot mess of resistors, capacitors, transistors, diodes, LED's, cable, screws, nuts, bolts, etc. they had stored in the connecting office. Seeing as all of the inventory had been stored in a storage unit for a few years in between Angiosonics going under and the creation of TriE, it was an undertaking. Especially since I was doing it by myself, one day a week, and we had little to no budget for things like organizational bins. Not only that, but a lot of the stuff wasn't even labeled, which made it more difficult for me because I was still learning the difference between a resistor and a capacitor, for crying out loud. And to top it off, those suckers are tiny!

So, to recap what I was working on for them at the beginning, it went as follows:

- Creating all policies and procedures
- Creating the HR procedures and implementing them
- Accounting
- Purchasing
- Creating an inventory system and implementing it

You might think that sounds like five different positions, but at the early stages of a business, it isn't really five full-time jobs. When in reality, it was probably more like two to three jobs I was working one day a week. Since I am a highly organized and efficient person, this workload wasn't a difficult feat for me to accomplish. But I realize this is very much not the norm. As the years progressed, and as we grew, I actually took on added positions in the company because five wasn't enough!

We stayed in our smaller office spaces for almost two years after I started working with them. But at that point, we had a few more employees, and it was getting cramped (plus I had no where to put the inventory!), so we found another larger space in the office complex just down the road and moved into it. Let me tell you, that was a pretty darn big undertaking!

Everybody who worked for the company, and was available, helped move all of the stuff over to the new location in one weekend. We were able to get it done, but it took a while to actually get the stuff organized, especially my precious inventory system. Even though my inventory system was still in the infant stages, I had a working system, and it was a bit chaotic for a while, trying to find everything. But since we had a larger space, I was able to spread out and actually block off a whole area of the warehouse just for inventory, which was a beautiful thing! The inventory system really started to come together in the new space, and as the years progressed, it grew in terms of product and efficiency. However, I was the only one performing the annual inventory for accuracy, and that sucked! It took me days to get it done, primarily because, at that point, I worked for them two days a week, but it was still only myself actually performing the inventory, and we had thousands of products. It was a mini version of hell whenever it came around each year. Of course, I was the one who implemented it, but it had to be implemented because of the level of facility we had become. By this, I mean that our facility had grown and changed throughout the years and now had become a completely different animal than it was when it began.

Since we were in the medical technology space, in order for us to gain the better contracts, we had to become ISO certified. So not only did we apply for the ISO 9001 but also for the ISO 3485, which was specific to the medical field. I not only assisted with figuring out how to apply for the ISO's but also created the majority of the documents, since I had been handling Policies and Procedures. And for those of you who don't know what ISO is, it's a quality control protocol that is used worldwide. This meant the governing bodies would come in and audit your company upon the initial application and see if you passed to become ISO certified. If you didn't, they would tell you where you failed, in great detail, and schedule a time to come back and re-audit you, to see if you have fixed the non-compliances.

Since I ran multiple departments, I was audited on a lot of different aspects, and we, as a company, passed the audit. This was fantastic, but it also meant the auditor would be back annually to audit two or three different departments, to ensure we were remaining compliant in order to keep our ISO certification. If we lost our ISO, that would mean large hospitals, labs, medical corporations, and the military contracts would drop us. So it was extremely important for us to remain compliant, and that meant documentation, documentation, documentation. It also meant we had to follow our policies and procedures down to a tee, so that is where the annual audit of the inventory system came into play. Not only had I done inventory before when I worked at Home Depot, BFS, and Diamond Hill, but I knew the only way to prove accuracy with my system was to perform an annual audit.

A little before the initial ISO audit took place, my youngest brother and his wife began working with us, also. My brother had just graduated with his Bachelor's in Marketing, and his wife had also just graduated and was looking for a full-time job. My brother began to work with Elizabeth full-time on the marketing aspect, and my sister-in-law began working part-time, a few days a week, on the receiving system. This was a system I hadn't had a chance to put into place yet, so it really helped. We collaborated on how the system should work, and she implemented it. We both wrote the documents for it and tweaked them as time went on, to match the changing procedure. She did the training for the employees, as to how the new receiving department was to operate, and sat back in the warehouse, checking stuff in and putting it in inventory for me. It was great to have them both working with us, and everything worked smoothly for a while, but all good things must come to an end. Both of them had grown tired of working with William because his demeanor towards employees, and just other people in general, was not so kind. He was similar to Don from my BFS days and tried to run with an iron fist, even if he hadn't been involved in the process and didn't know what he was talking about. Neither my brother nor his wife are fond of being yelled and screamed at, so they both ended up leaving the company for other opportunities, which was sad, but I understood where they were coming from. Of course, that meant I took over the Receiving department, just to add one more job to my plate.

Getting back to William, though, and the ultimate demise of the company, he had a way of driving people away. At first, he was really great to work with; he liked me because we had a history and he knew I was a hard worker and a problem solver. I could get shit done and not only didn't complain but found answers to problems so I didn't have to bother them with menial stuff they didn't have time for.

I remember that he pulled me aside before I gave birth to my daughter and told me how much he appreciated me, and that if I kept up with the pace at which I had been working, I would really go somewhere in my career. He seemed to look at me like a mentee that he was proud of, which was really nice, but my success had absolutely nothing to do with him or anything that he had taught me. This is simply my nature and many years of diversifying through many other unrelated jobs.

The downfall in our relationship began when I had my daughter. William wanted me to work for them full-time, and I told him that was never the deal and that I wasn't interested because I wanted to be home to raise my children. Once they were in school, then that would be something I would consider. He didn't like that answer and told me I was throwing my life away. But before this conversation, I should tell you I was finishing my undergrad when I started working with them, and while I was still in school, I asked both William and my father what the probability was for a raise once I graduated. My father told me I would have to take it up with William because he didn't want to show favoritism. So I had a talk with William, and he agreed that, once I graduated, I would be bumped up to $20 an hour, from my current $15 an hour. Once I graduated from college, I became pregnant with my daughter almost immediately. I asked William for the raise we had agreed upon, and that was when he decided to pull the "full-time" request upon me. When I told him no, he got really mad and, again, began to tell me I was wasting my life, and the only way he would honor the raise was if I agreed to work full-time. I, again, informed him that was never part of the deal and that I deserved the raise because of all of the hard work I had been putting into the creation of this company, as well as the fact that we agreed I would get the raise once I graduated. This ended up becoming a heated discussion, and I had to bring my father in as the deciding vote. Since he was there for the initial conversation about the raise happening upon my graduation, he sided with me and told William he couldn't add a stipulation to the raise, after the fact. Therefore, the raise was implemented, and that was what I ended up making the rest of the years I was at TriE. I asked for another raise a few years later but was denied because I was told I wasn't worth it, even though I was still handling multiple departments by myself. If you can't tell, that still irks me. It did, as efficiently as I did them, for what they were paying me. But as I have gotten older, I've begun to fully realize my worth and fight more for appropriate compensation.

After I had my daughter, I still worked for them two days a week, but I did take two weeks off. I still answered questions over the phone, and I could get some minor stuff done from home during that brief time. But then it was back to work because there was nobody else handling those departments. So to recap, at this point, I was handling all of the following departments:

- Accounting
- Purchasing
- Receiving
- Inventory
- HR
- Documentation (although we had brought on some new people that were helping with a lot of the documents)

I'm sure a lot of you are having a difficult time wrapping your brain around how I did all of this in only two days a week (and they weren't even eight-hour days, most of the time) but I did. This is because I can just quickly transfer from one task to the next. In fact, I really love the challenge of multiple jobs within one company because I can see how all of the processes flow together like a river. It just makes sense in my brain, especially when it comes to writing documentation. If I have been running the departments, I know exactly what I'm supposed to write the documentation on because I know how the system works.

This could have been a beautiful thing for the long haul because I was good at it, and I liked working with my dad. We have similar personalities, work ethics, and drives, so that helps. We also look at numbers the same way, but I can tell you he is not nearly as organized as I am. He might tell you that he is, but his desk always looked like a paper tornado had hit it, whereas mine did not, *ever*.

After eight years of working with them and fighting with William the majority of the time, I decided I had had enough of fighting with him and fighting for my employees. I would throw myself in between William and any of the employees he decided to verbally beat down upon because not only was I in charge of HR but he couldn't fire me, as much as he wanted to when I went toe to toe with him. I don't agree with people being treated the way he was treating people, and I would be damned if I was going to let him if I had a say in it. And I did. He and my dad got into many yelling matches throughout the years at work, also, which was kind of embarrassing, to be honest. But the thing with William was he thought that, since he was 50% owner, he could do whatever he wanted without running it by my father and them both agreeing. My father had grown tired of that, especially because William was continually making decisions that were harming the company's future because we couldn't handle the promises he was making to clients. The yelling matches went outside as the years progressed, but William would still get in my face, which was extremely unprofessional. He would also yell and scream at his daughters, both of whom worked for us at the time, and tell them they were stupid, couldn't do anything right, and were a waste of space. The worst part is that they took the abuse from him, but I am simply not wired that way.

I remember there was one yelling match that was so bad William cocked his arm back to hit me. He had come into my inventory space while I was working on inventory to yell at me about something, and I simply just didn't have the time or the patience for his bullshit, so I told him to get out of my space while I was working, or he was going to ruin my count. He was yelling about something, when his face started turning red because he was so mad, and that's when he cocked his fist back. I told him to go ahead and hit me because I would be more than happy to call the police and have him arrested for assault. In fact, I may have taunted him a bit to get him to do it because, at that point, I would have loved nothing more than to get him removed in handcuffs because he had become such a horrible person to work with, for every-body. I think that brought him back to reality, and he put his fist down and walked away. It was at that point, I knew I couldn't keep doing this, even though I was working with my father and liked working with him. William was making everybody's lives miserable, and life is simply just too short for that nonsense.

I had already made the decision that I wasn't going to stay for the long haul anymore around December of 2012, but I had to find some replacement income because, at this point, I was a single mother, and it was my only source of income. Around the same time, my dad and William had their final falling out, and William decided he wanted to sell the company, or he would leave and leave my dad with all of the debts. So he began looking for buyers and found one who was inter-ested. At the end of December, they announced at the holiday party that we would be embarking upon a new partnership that would really help the company grow to new heights. I knew that was bullshit, but

I also knew what was really going on because the other owner of the company happened to be my father and we talked regularly. He didn't see another way out of the situation because of how they had set up the company at the onset and how much debt was personally tied to him. So they brought on the new partners who were set to acquire us slowly over the next year and keep my father on to help with the transition.

When I first met Pransu, I knew I didn't like him. There was something off about him, and he had a similar air about him that William had. I hate to say he didn't like women, but it was obvious he didn't think the workforce was for women.

He brought us all into a meeting the first day he was at the office (before he knew anything about our processes or how we operated) and sat us down to have a talk. He was telling us that he was going to keep things the same for now because he wanted to see how things worked, but he did tell me he had his own person for purchasing, so they were slowly going to be taking that over and that he wanted my contacts. I was pissed off and told him that was great, but it took me years to create these relationships with my vendors, and they were a picky breed, so I didn't think that was a wise decision. He didn't really like that answer and basically told me I needed to stay in my place. Good luck with that, buddy!

It was at this point that I knew I was going to leave for good, and it was happening soon. He brought in one girl to try to learn my purchasing process, and his assistant, which was his son, wanted to learn my accounting process. So in good form, I taught them how I operated those departments and the documentation required to keep that up because that was integral to keeping our ISO certification. This, coincidentally, was one of the main reasons why they wanted to acquire us, since they didn't have ISO for any of their other businesses and had been unable to obtain it. The long and short of this story is that I did end up leaving in March of 2013, and they tried to get the next girl (because the first girl who tried to learn my purchasing procedures quit within two days) to take over all of my positions, and she threw up her hands inside of two weeks and walked out. She said there was no way that one person could handle all that I was in charge of. She couldn't figure it out and left. They called me multiple times after I left and asked me for help with different aspects of different positions. I told them I left copious documentation, as to my processes, and trained them on the processes, but since they still couldn't figure it out, I would be willing to come and help on a contract basis, for more money. They balked at that offer because they wanted me to do it for free. I told them no, and they never asked again.

I was told they tried two other people after the initial girl walked away, and nobody could figure out how I did it, so most of those departments just fell by the wayside, and when they got audited by ISO for those departments, they failed. It was really sad for me because I worked so hard to make it a streamlined, well-operating machine, and it worked beautifully when I did it, but maybe there just aren't enough people out there who can handle that many things at once. Either way, it was hard for me to fully let it go because I had spent so much blood, sweat, and tears on the company, and it was my father's. But it simply just is what it is, and time moved on.

**35**

**What I Learned**

★ Creating something out of nothing is something I really enjoy

★ I am much more organized than I ever gave myself credit for

★ I love creating documentation!

★ Doing inventory is very cathartic for me, and I enjoy it

★ Purchasing is all about creating relationships to give and get the best deal

★ My father and I work very well together, most of the time, and he taught me a lot

★ I do not respond well to verbal abuse and will not put up with it

★ HR is a tricky animal, but I enjoyed learning the idiosyncrasies of it

★ I love the challenge of working multiple seemingly unrelated departments

★ I am a better problem solver than I ever gave myself credit for

★ I can get a ridiculous amount of work done in a very short amount of time when left to my own devices

★ It's hard to let go of your baby and watch it crash and burn when you no longer have anything to do with it

★ Any partnership that is truly fifty-fifty is doomed to be problematic and most likely go up in flames. One person must have slightly more skin in the game in order to make it work out well

# Moonlight Bakery

As a person who was diagnosed with Celiac Disease back in 1986, attention to food has always been a big part of my world. It wasn't really a choice but rather a necessity for survival. So, being "gluten-free" wasn't a fad when I got diagnosed. In fact, I lived with it successfully for over twenty years before it ever caught on in the mainstream.

I had to figure out, on my own, what I could eat that was gluten-free. I learned this through reading ingredients—every ingredient—and knowing what the ingredients were code for. This is the same skill I have taught my son, who also has Celiac Disease, and it has also served him well.

Since I had such a difficult time finding things that were gluten-free out in the world, I resorted to creating my own goodies. It first started with the peanut butter cookies my mom made for me as a child because she didn't know another kind of treat to make me. I don't know the full story behind the peanut butter cookies, but she did tell me that she found the recipe in one of her old books and tweaked it a little. They were delicious and only contained three ingredients, to boot! When I owned the bakery, these were one of my biggest sellers, along with my carrot cake and cheesecake cups.

But I am jumping the gun here and haven't told you how the bakery formed in the first place, so let's go back.

Since I had been making my gluten-free goodies for years, people had begun to ask for them for holidays, dinner parties, gifts for their friends, etc. And I was more than happy to do it, but there started to become a point where I was spending a lot of money on the ingredients for treats, and I couldn't really afford to keep doing it.

My sister-in-law and I had a conversation about it one day, because she also loves to bake, and discussed the possibility of creating our own bakery. At first, the idea was to make it a bakery that had a lot of gluten-free baked goods, also, but she likes to bake more in the traditional sense, with wheat flour. I wasn't as keen on that idea because of the cross-contamination issue, as well as the possibility someone could inadvertently get a non-gluten-free goodie and get sick.

At first, we agreed to try it as a joint venture, and we both brought recipes to the table. She was good with the flavored breads such as pumpkin cream cheese swirl, banana bread, zucchini bread, etc., and I was better with the cookies and muffins. We both worked on creating a gluten-free sandwich bread because the cupcakes were easy, in our book.

So once we had the recipe stock to pull from, then we had to come up with a name. We went through a lot of options, as any entrepreneur will tell you, because we were trying to decide the best fit for our product and what we were doing. The term "moonlighting" kept coming up because this was something we were doing on the side. My sister-in-law had a full-time job, and I was being a stay-at-home mom and working two part-time jobs, so I didn't have time for anything full-time. Due to the circumstances in which the bakery was created, Moonlight Bakery just seemed like a good fit.

I did an entity search and found no other Moonlight Bakery in our state or in any other state, so that clinched the name. I can tell you that, after we were in business for about a year, I got a phone call from a pizza joint named Moonlight Pizza, who said they wanted to sue us for having a name too close to theirs. I informed them we were a gluten-free bakery, and they were a pizza place and that the word Moonlight wasn't trademarked, so good luck. They left us alone after that, but it was weird.

I had some experience with creating websites, but not a ton, so I asked my brother for help. He also worked full-time (the same brother who worked with me at TriE) but was also running his own business on the side and trying to build that up. He was in the ecommerce business for electronics, at the time, so I knew he would know the best way to build a website. Therefore, he is the one who taught me HTML code. Luckily, we don't have to use that much anymore for websites because we have this awesome thing called WordPress, but that wasn't around back in 2009, when I was building the Moonlight Bakery website.

So I built the website and had to keep it up, as well as keep up with coupon codes and events. But I also created all of the recipe cards and nutrition facts, which are not only very important to me but technically are required on any and all food products. A lot of smaller companies don't realize this, so they don't do it, but I like to do things by the book so I don't inadvertently get into trouble for something as small as not having proper labeling. I also handled the books and taxes, so I had my hands in quite a few pots. My favorite part of all of it was the creation of new recipes and talking to people about gluten-free products, but the rest of it, I could have done without.

We decided to start by selling at the farmers' market, but the big one wouldn't let us in because they had too many bakers. I tried to get them to understand that we were selling gluten-free baked goods, which was something they didn't have, but this was in a time when food products being gluten-free wasn't widely known yet, so they had no idea what I was referring to, even when I explained it. Therefore, we decided to go to a smaller farmer's market that was closer for both of us, and they welcomed us with open arms.

The first few times we went, we were baking out of my house. But not too long after that, when we tried to become a certified kitchen, I realized we couldn't bake out of there because I had a dog, and that was on the no-no list. So, we both started looking for alternative options, and my partner came up with a great solution! She somehow met up with the owner of a Dinner Savvy, which is one of those places where they have the recipes and all of the ingredients prepped so you can create the recipes at the location, and then just bring the dishes home and pop them in the oven. The owner didn't use her kitchen very often because there wasn't a whole lot of baking or cooking going on, so for $10 an hour, she was willing to let us use it whenever we needed. Plus, she had a commercial dishwasher, which was awesome, so that was a huge bonus!

That meant we had to drive there and haul our stuff, but she did clear off a shelf for us to store items, which made things a little bit easier. Ultimately, we started selling at the farmers' market and doing home deliveries in the beginning. But that changed throughout the course of the business.

Eventually, my sister-in-law didn't want to do it anymore because it took up too much time, and she wanted to focus on her full-time job, plus gluten-free baked goods wasn't her passion, it was mine. I understood that completely, and since we hadn't made any profit at that time, she just bowed out of the company and signed over her half to me. At that point, I was the sole owner of Moonlight Bakery.

I had been working on creating the relationships and going to any and all meetings that had to do with Celiac Disease so I could get the information out about our products. By doing so, I was starting to become known in the Celiac community as the only independent gluten-free bakery. The only other place that was local where one could get freshly baked gluten-free goodies was at the Whole Foods in Chapel Hill, where Lee worked. He had developed Celiac and began to start baking gluten-free goods on Tuesdays. I'm not sure about the entire deal, but I know he was allowed to use the kitchen one day a week, in which he thoroughly cleaned and sanitized it prior to baking, and then the next day was the day when anybody could swing by and grab what he was able to bake. His morning glory muffins were my favorite! But after gluten-free started to become a thing, he helped Whole Foods start the Gluten Free Bakehouse in Morrisville, which did production-run baking to distribute to all of the local Whole Foods, and they stopped making my morning glory muffins. Oddly enough, at the beginning of his Gluten Free Bakehouse journey, I was part of the taste panel for their new gluten-free goods, but also ran Moonlight Bakery at the time. I don't think he knew that, or he probably would have kicked me off for being a conflict of interest. I didn't argue, though, because I got to try his new stuff for free, and I love free! Especially when it's gluten-free because this stuff gets really expensive.

Eventually, I was able to get into a few restaurants and even the Durham Bulls ballpark. Not only that, but I got the Durham Bulls to start carrying gluten-free beer, and they had me go around to each vendor and tell them what products were gluten-free and what products weren't so they could properly advertise. I did that by reading the ingredients on everything! Which none of them knew how to do because they were never taught, nor did they know what a lot of the ingredients derived from. This is one of my superpowers because I have been doing it for so long that it's basically second nature, so it was a walk in the park for me.

Dinner Savvy started keeping some of our baked goods in the cooler at the front of the store, also, so patrons could purchase our stuff even when we weren't there. I know I appreciated that because it meant I didn't have to be there to sell product.

Overall, the biggest issues for me became time and money. Some of the restaurants that were carrying my stuff didn't regularly pay me on time. So I ended up spending more time than I really had trying to track down the money they owed me for my baked goods which they had already sold. I found that larger companies have policies, and it doesn't matter to them if you are a small business, they are going to pay when their terms say, even if you had "Due Upon Receipt" terms upon your original contract. And then there were some companies that stiffed me altogether, which I despise.

Another company found me, because they heard about what I was doing, and asked me to help them create a gluten-free menu for a new restaurant they were opening in the area, as well as provide them with gluten-free baked goods for the restaurant. I was extremely excited about that opportunity, and it was going really well until two days before they opened. The restaurant, Sparions (which is no longer in business here), even asked me to create gluten-free hamburger buns, sliders, and custom muffins for them, which I did. I went through their potential menu and their ingredients with a fine-tooth comb and worked with the chef to explain the best practices to avoid cross-contamination. We worked on this for a little over three months, and they were supposed to be giving me the first order at least a week prior to them opening so I would have time to produce the items they decided they wanted. I called multiple times when I hadn't heard from them, and nobody responded until two days before they opened. During that phone call, I was told they decided they weren't going to do anything gluten-free and that they weren't going to pay me for the time I had spent with them to create it. Needless to say, they ended up high on my shit list, and I haven't been back to the place since.

That left a really bad taste in my mouth, along with the other companies that were extremely slow to pay. I also refused to cut corners on my ingredients because my ingredients were what made my products not only good but better for you than the alternatives. I used applesauce instead of oil, local honey, organic cane sugar, and ground flaxseed sometimes instead of eggs. None of these ingredients are cheap, but they made my products not only gluten-free but unique. The quality I put into my food was the main reason people asked me for my baked goods before I ever started the bakery. Because none of them were required to eat gluten-free. So if I started cutting corners on my ingredients, I wasn't being true to myself, my product, or my company, and I wasn't okay with that. On top of the two aforementioned issues, I was going through a divorce and had recently become a single mother. Between all three of those issues, something just had to give, and I decided it was time to shut down the bakery after only being open for two years. My regular customers were sad, and so was I, but I just didn't have the bandwidth to keep it going, and my life situation had changed. It was a sad day when I shut down Moonlight Bakery in 2011, but I learned a lot, and I wouldn't trade the experience for anything.

**36**

**What I Learned**

★ How to perform an entity search when starting a business

★ The ins and outs of creating EIN's, sales and use tax ID's, as well as paying business taxes

★ How to create a website in HTML code

★ How much I dislike writing HTML code

★ The local laws about where you can and cannot bake outside of a commercial kitchen environment

★ What I won't skimp on with regard to business operating costs

★ How to get in as a vendor with restaurants

★ That I don't like selling at farmers' markets because it's a lot of setup and breakdown, and the weather is unpredictable

★ Sometimes, the best decision is to end something you love when it is no longer sustainable

# Irregardless Catering

In high school, one of my close friends waited tables for a local restaurant called Irregardless, in downtown Raleigh. I used to love going there because they were well known for their vegetarian dishes and fresh ingredients, which was not something you ran across much in the 90s. My friend had moved away many years before but came back every now and then to work and see her family.

It just happened to be that she came back in the summer of 2011 to visit and pick up a few shifts at Irregardless while she was here. She and I were talking at my house one day about the fact that I could really use a side gig to help with my bills and feeding the kids. She told me she knew their catering department could really use some more bodies and that it wasn't a permanent or regular thing, so it might be a good fit for me.

She reached out to Stacy, the head of catering, who then gave me a call, to do a phone interview. She hired me on the spot and told me they sometimes had four to five events a month but that it varied. Her right-hand lady, Angela, would be in charge of scheduling and would text me when they had events coming up, to see if I could work them. This was a beautiful schedule for me because, if I knew ahead of time, then I could try to find somebody to watch my kids so I could work. And to top it off, they let us bring home leftovers, which helped with my food budget. Bonus!

Stacy told me they paid $15 an hour, and that worked really well for me. However, the first paycheck I got from them showed they were only paying me $13.85. I was really confused, as to what was going on, so I reached out to Stacy about it. She told me the pay was $15 an hour, but that was before they took taxes out, so really it was $13.85 per hour. I told her that still didn't make sense because the paycheck showed them taking taxes out of the $13.85, so that meant they were taxing me twice. She said that was just how they did it and that I didn't understand how the taxes worked. Um, yes, I did! Especially because I worked in Accounting for TriE for almost eight years and did my own books and taxes for Moonlight Bakery. I didn't want to get into an argument with her about it, but it really ticked me off that they were taking advantage of people like that and not even telling the truth about it. But I needed the work, so I just dropped it.

This was right after the Great Recession hit and the economy was still recovering. So I understand it was difficult for businesses to make any money during this time. But it was also hard for us, as employees or contract workers, to make any money, either. And a lot of us have families to feed, like myself.

If I weren't in desperate need of money to help pay the bills (because at this point, I was still a single mother only working the one part-time job, so we were living on approximately $800 a month), then I would have told her where to shove it. I greatly detest being underestimated, especially when it comes to money, simple math, and taxes, which is exactly what she was doing. Of course, I realized later that it wasn't of her own accord, but rather it was the owner's way of getting around paying us more. This is a shocker to you, I know!

Unfortunately, I have seen it happen all over the restaurant industry, so it's almost an industry standard to take advantage of workers. This is one of the reasons why so many food industry people move around to different locations. Some places take less advantage of employees and pay better money, but they are pretty few and far between. I am hoping that will continue to change for the better, as the more the knowledge about how food service workers are continually treated is put out there.

Their catering division operated out of the basement of the restaurant, so we were completely separate, with the exception of having to go upstairs to the kitchen to get our food for events. We packed the trucks out of the basement from the pull list Mary and Angela created. Mary was Angela's mother and had worked with Irregardless for more years than I know. She was the most organized person, besides myself, that I have ever run across, and she was fantastic at creating pull lists. Mary was the one who taught me what a hotbox was because I had never heard that term before.

The basic gist of what we did for events was to pack up the van, drive to the location of the event, set up the tables with our linens, chafers, decorations, and the food, serve food and sometimes beverages, clean up the event, drive back to the restaurant, unpack the van, put all of the dirty dishes in the dumbwaiter and send it upstairs to the dish pit, and then leave. Sounds simple, right? That wasn't always the case, that's for sure!

Using my staging skill from The Cookie Store, from much earlier in my work history, really came in handy here. Not only did that job teach me how to make food pleasing to the eye, but the interior designer background with Bell and Associates didn't hurt, either. Both places taught me how to stage properly, as well as how to make things more aesthetically pleasing and balanced. These skills are very useful in the catering industry because you want your layouts to look beautiful and inviting but also to flow well for the most efficient service time.

Sometimes, we had a bar, which was my favorite part (and they paid me $20 an hour to do this, as opposed to just catering), since I used to bartend, way back in the day. So after the first few events, when they realized I could bartend, they started using me as their regular bartender for events, which I liked just fine. That meant I got to stand behind the bar and come up with random creations and talk to guests, but I didn't have to kill my arms carrying around heavy trays the whole event. The interesting caveat with bartending at catered events is that it is never a full bar, but more like a crapshoot. You never know what you're going to get, in terms of alcohol, when you walk into an event, so you have to be good at coming up with drinks on the fly, which just happens to be one of my areas of expertise.

I loved this aspect of catering because it meant I got to be creative and work on flavor profiles, most of the time. I do recall a wedding where I was the head bartender and, the only alcohol they provided was Fireball. This was for a wedding of over 200 people, and the only thing the bride and groom provided was Fireball! I found out it was because it was their favorite alcohol, which is all great and wonderful because it is your wedding. But, and here is the *but*, you invited over 200 people to your wedding and presumed they all love Fireball as much as you do. Or at all, for that matter. Good luck with all that! They did provide some juices and club soda. This was the worst wedding of my catering career because there wasn't much I could do with it.

I did send somebody out to get some Sprite so I could mix it with cranberry juice and the Fireball. It turned out pretty good and worked well for all of those guests that didn't want to shoot Fireball because it tasted slightly sweet, with a hint of tartness rounded out by a quick hint of spice. It was a pretty good blend, if I do say so myself! But the lesson here is simply this: It may be your wedding, but please have the common decency to provide things that other people may like because it really isn't all about you.

Overall, I enjoyed working with the Irregardless catering crew because it was sporadic, I got in some exercise, got to use my brain sometimes to be creative, and the crew was tight. There weren't many of us, and we were an all-women crew, so we became a tighter niche. Ultimately, I didn't leave catering with Irregardless, but later on in this story, you will see where they moved me to a different position.

**37**

**What I Learned**

★ There are jobs you can work sporadically that work with a single parent's schedule

★ What the hell a hotbox is!

★ You get to bring home leftovers from catering events

★ Working with an all-women crew can be very enjoyable if you are all hard workers

★ Bartending weddings is much different than bartending at a bar or restaurant

★ You have to pay close attention to what people tell you and what they are actually paying you because sometimes people are full of shit

# North Carolina Museum of Natural Sciences (Volunteer)

Around the same time I started working for Irregardless, I began to volunteer at the Science Museum. I had been taking my children to this museum since Reese was about six months old. The museum was a little over a mile from our house, and I could walk there; plus, it was free. Up until I had children, I had never visited it, which is really sad because it's such a fantastic museum.

In April of 2012, they opened the NRC (Nature Research Center), which was the new wing of the museum that had four additional floors, making the museum a total of eight floors, which is pretty darn huge! The NRC grand opening was forty-eight hours long and was run primarily by volunteers, and some contractors, which I found out later. I loved volunteering with them, so I inquired as to how I could do more. I was told I would need to contact Tullie, who was in charge of the volunteers, to get on the list, and then they would send me emails for events when they became available. I knew I wouldn't be able to volunteer for all of the events, but I loved the museum so much and my kids and I had spent so much time there that I wanted to help out whenever I could.

After volunteering for a few events, one of the employees I had gotten to know during story time and Meet the Animals, Sunny, told me I should really sign up to volunteer in a specific department because I was a great volunteer. So I went to the orientation and heard about all of the volunteer opportunities. Upon hearing them all, I decided I wanted to create an educational cart in the cart program with Steph. She and I talked, and I threw out a few ideas for a cart I could create and run. She loved the idea of the dinosaur cart because she didn't really have anybody running one at the time.

My idea was to create a cart with different models of dinosaurs, other animals, and humans, to show how Paleontologists determine dinosaur characteristics based on our current knowledge about various species that exist today. Both she and I gathered different specimens and reading material to create the cart. She had the art department create some visual materials for me, and one of the volunteers in the Paleo lab, Hugo, created a baby dinosaur in an egg for me to use as a touchable example. It was a pretty cool cart, and people really seemed to like it.

I could come in whenever I wanted, to run the cart, but there were certain areas of the museum that had more traffic, so she preferred if I picked one of those higher trafficked areas to position myself.

I loved running this cart because it was a great feeling for me to see the excitement in children's eyes when I taught them something they didn't already know, especially about dinosaurs! I really wish I could have done it for more hours and more often because I loved being able to teach again, like when I was a TA. But I only ended up doing it for a little less than a year, about once or twice a month because that was all the time I could spare. My daughter had begun preschool, but it was only three hours a day, so that was my window of time. Not only that, but not too long after I started volunteering with the cart program, another department came to me and asked me if I wanted to get paid to work at the museum. This eventually led me to stop volunteering because they began paying me instead, which I couldn't argue with.

**38**

**What I Learned**

★ I enjoy getting to use my brain to create fun learning activities

★ Teaching people about science is a passion of mine

★ Working with the museum to create carts can be a long process, but a lot of fun

★ If you show initiative at something you love, and do it for free, a lot of times, people will then start paying you for it

★ I love working at the museum!

# North Carolina Museum
# of Natural Sciences
# (Contractor)

unning carts at the Museum was what ended up gaining me the attention of another department that just happened to be willing to pay me to be there. I was approached and asked if I would be interested in working the large events not as a volunteer but as a contractor. What that meant was that I would help with setting up the event the day prior, and then help run the event and the volunteers, as well as break it down. And they would pay me for it, to boot! Of course, I said yes because I loved working at the museum and getting paid to do something you enjoy is even better than doing it for free.

The pay for this wasn't spectacular, either, but the museum is run half by donations and half by government funding, so it was to be expected. They told me contractors get paid $13.85 an hour, and they feed us dinner during setup, as well as lunch and dinner the day of the event. At this point, I wasn't arguing with free food because I could use all the help I could get. I was still a struggling single parent and on food stamps at this point in time, so any free meals I could get, I took advantage of.

The first event they asked me to work was, and still is, one of my favorites: Bug Fest! This large event takes place the third Saturday of every September, and it draws a huge crowd. Setting up requires pulling all of the event materials from the cage down on the A level, as well as gathering up tablecloths from the "Scary Place" on the B level (both levels are basement levels that are not accessible to guests). We always have rental tables dropped off for us—the huge heavy wood tables that are a beast to move. But once you figure out the system to pull the legs out first and use your knee to kick the table up and then throw it down, you're good to go. One of the employees taught me that during my first event, and it has helped me ever since.

Usually, the setup day runs from 9:00 a.m. to anywhere until 11:00 p.m., but that really all depends on the event and the staff we have in place. The day of the event, we usually show up at 6:30 a.m., and we can leave as soon as we are done breaking down. So while this depends on the breakdown staff, we usually get out of there somewhere around 8:00 p.m. now. When I first started, we didn't get out of there until closer to 10:00 p.m., but the systems have been streamlined and honed now so that they are more efficient.

Kari is the head of this department and is fantastic with her organizational skills. And she would have to be to pull this off! When I started, she had two other people who helped her in the department, Miranda and Bonnie. A few years after I started with them, though, Bonnie left to take a position at a botanical garden, which was a great move for her, but she is now back with the museum. Although, now she's at the Prairie Ridge Ecostation, in a different part of Raleigh. Miranda is still with Kari and helps her run the department very smoothly. In between, they had another person, Bradley, helping them for about a year. But he decided he wanted to go back to grad school and left. Now they have Hugo, who also worked with me in Special Exhibits, taking over that roll. They make a good team, from my perspective. Of course, I have no idea what goes on behind the scenes because I am only there to help with the big events. The events they have contracted me for are:

- Bug Fest (every third Saturday in September)
- Paleo Palooza (every November, but no longer an event)
- Astronomy Days (the last weekend in January, and runs both days)
- Darwin Day (every February around Valentine's Day)
- Herp Day (every March)
- SciTech Expo (every April)
- Scavenger Hunts (whenever groups request them, they need people to run them)
- Adult Nights (these are newer events they are having every two to three months on a Friday night)
- Solar Eclipse (contracted me out to a third party to run a program during the solar eclipse in August of 2017)

I love working these events, but the older I get, the more tiring they are for me. That may actually have more to do with the fact that I regularly sit in front of a computer for all of my contract work and businesses and am not as active as I was a few years ago. I still contract for these events with them, and I still love it! I have no plans to stop any time soon because it keeps me connected to the museum, which I greatly adore, even if I never want to work full-time there.

**39**

**What I Learned**

★ Creating a special event and getting the staff to run it efficiently is a much larger task than I was ever aware of

★ Throwing tables around is actually kind of fun, at least the first few times

★ The museum has a lot of hidden nooks and crannies I never saw prior to this job

★ I really like the Special Events staff and how well they work together

★ Even if the pay isn't exceptional, I will work for free food (although, I am pretty picky about what the food is)

# North Carolina Museum
# of Natural Sciences
# (Special Exhibits)

ot too long after I started working with Special Events, I got approached about working in Special Exhibits and getting paid to do so. Granted, the pay was $9 an hour, which was beyond horrible for me, but it was better than nothing. Not only that, but they made the schedule a month in advance, so all I had to do was give them my availability, and they would work me in wherever they could. I couldn't argue with this because it was a department I hadn't worked in before, and they were offering to pay me, albeit meagerly. Beggars can't be choosers, so I took it with enthusiasm!

The Special Exhibit hall was where the rotating paid exhibits went. So anybody who came in had to have a ticket for entrance to be accepted. Sometimes, I would be a ticket taker and tell guests the rules of the exhibit, which all changed depending on the exhibit. Other times, I would be a roamer, which was my preference because it meant I got to roam around the exhibit hall and talk to guests, which I really enjoyed. Plus, when it was really slow, I was notorious for wearing my step tracker and walking the hall as much as possible for mileage so I worked in my exercise.

The first exhibit I ever worked was the Titanic, and it was fabulous! If you have never seen this exhibit, you've got to check it out. I believe there are six or seven different roaming Titanic exhibits, but they are all similar. I really liked working the last room of the exhibit on this one because each person got a boarding pass upon entrance, with a name on it of an actual passenger. In the last room, they got to see whether they lived or died and what part of the ship they were staying on. This could be a very emotional experience for a lot of people, especially those who had family members lost on the Titanic. This room really hit home, not only with the guests but with me. It reminded me that life is short and we never really know what the future will hold. That always hits home with me. Either way, though, it was a pretty cool experience!

I stayed in this department until another full-time corporate job plucked me in the summer of 2013, but we will get to that shortly.

**40**

**What I Learned**

★ A lot more goes into creating a special exhibit than I ever knew

★ You work at a museum because you love it, not because you want to make good money

★ The museum is a really good place to work, and very diverse

# Rocky Top Catering

Since I was already at the museum, I figured I would try to get some more gigs there because I loved it so much. The next natural place for me to venture into was the catering department because of my background in food. I had worked at enough restaurants to know this world pretty well. And since I had already started working some catering gigs with Irregardless, I figured this would be an easy segue. Especially because I was starting to know the ins and outs of the museum, also.

Both of the cafés in the museum are run by Rocky Top Catering, which is a company in and of itself offsite. But they got the contract to be the exclusive caterers at the museum, as well as run the two cafés. Therefore, the manager at the main café in the NRC, the Daily Planet Café, is who I wanted to speak with. I went down to speak with Seth, who was one of the two managers, and he said they would give me a call. But, of course, they never did.

Lo and behold, though, there was an ad placed in March of 2013 for catering staff needed for Rocky Top through their main division, which was at the 1705 hub offsite. So, I applied and got an interview with Rachel. She hired me on the spot because of my background and people skills, or at least that is what she told me. She also liked that I seemed responsible, which was true and still is, so I suppose I had that going for me. They were going to start me off at $12 an hour, plus leftover food to take home from events. Since I was already working at the museum, she gave me access to sign up for the events there, which not all catering staff had the availability to do.

While, technically, Rachel was the one who initially hired me, Seth and I ended up becoming good work friends, and he used me a lot for the events there. The reasoning was because I was older, more responsible, more reliable, had bartending experience, and was the only person on staff who also worked for the museum.

I ended up doing the same things for Rocky Top as I did for Irregardless, but I worked a lot more for Rocky Top than for Irregardless. Even though Irregardless still paid me more, Rocky Top gave me more shifts. What made it even easier was that, a lot of the time, the Rocky Top shifts would start right after I was wrapping up my shift in Special Exhibits, so all I had to do was walk across the bridge and change clothes. You really can't beat that!

In very little time, I became one of the main bartenders and worked the big parties, including their huge New Year's Eve party every year, where I systematically got my ass handed to me, along with the other bartenders. This party takes up all four floors of the NRC and caps at 1,000 people. It is all you can drink and eat with admission, so people get a little bit crazy with the bars. But it was a lesson for me in learning you have to have a good team to help you pull it off.

I loved working the shifts at the museum, but at this point, I had left TriE, so I was trying to make up more money to pay bills and pay off some debt. So, I started to pick up a lot of shifts for the offsite gigs, also.

I can tell you that I didn't like these gigs nearly as much! Part of that might have something to do with the fact that we would have to show up at the 1705 location (because that is where the kitchen and catering hub was) to load the van. Then, at the end of the night, we would have to go *back* to 1705 and unload the van, as well as wash *all* of the dishes from the event. I absolutely *hated* this aspect of it. With Irregardless, there was always a dishwasher, or we would just send the dumbwaiter upstairs with the dirty dishes for the dish crew to take care of in the morning. But that was not how they had things structured at 1705, and nobody liked it. So they paid me less per hour than Irregardless, but I also had to wash dishes. If you're thinking this didn't sound like such a hot deal, that was my thought process, too.

But this job gave me the flexibility to sign up for shifts based on my availability, which was crucial to my life, at this point, because I was a single mother. I could really only work when I didn't have my kids or when I could find somebody to watch them for free. When I could find somebody to watch them for free, I would bring home a lot of extra food and pay them in food. Most of the people who helped me out really liked that, so they were more amenable to watching the kids at no cost.

Ultimately, if everything would've stayed the way it was at the museum, I would have stayed with them longer than the two and a half years that I did, but that just wasn't the case. Seth had a wife and a young son and very rarely had a day off, so he asked to be switched, to just manage the café instead so that he could have some family time. Work-life balance was something I was really working on myself during this point of my life, so I completely understood where he was coming from. But it just wasn't the same without him on the catering side of things.

He was very organized, like me, and was good at running a staff effectively. People respected him and did what he asked. What we got as a replacement were two women who liked to scream and yell and tell people they were idiots. Now, in case you have forgotten, this sort of management style doesn't really work with my personality. Especially since I was older and more responsible than both of these women—that made it even harder for me to respect them. It was at this point that I started seeing some of the regular employees asking to work offsite and not at the museum.

This is where the decline began for me. They started to bring in more staff that was younger and less experienced. Not only that, but I found that the younger staff they were bringing in all had the same mentality. This mentality included staying on their cell phones, very little work ethic, and expecting something for nothing. I hate to stereotype, but sometimes they exist for a reason; this group I'm referring to are known as Millennials. Please note that I know there are always exceptions to the rule, we just didn't have any of the exceptions in this particular situation.

Because I was one of the older employees and worked at the museum, also, they had me train new employees about where things went and the setup they preferred there. This was fine, but they didn't pay me extra for that. In fact, the only raise I ever got was when I pinned Seth down, after I had been there a year, and told him I deserved a raise for my annual review. They didn't actually do annual reviews, but I told him that was standard operating procedure and, unless there was some reason why he didn't think I deserved a raise, then that was the least he could do. He agreed and bumped me up to $13 an hour, so now I was making more than most of the other catering staff sans managers.

Although, $13 is nothing to write home about, it was still better than nothing, and I knew it wouldn't always be like that, so I took what I could get.

But I digress again! The end came in the summer of 2015, when they had three female managers on site, for some unknown reason. The event wasn't even a big event, so one manager would have been more than sufficient. At the end of the night, when we were cleaning up, the three couldn't agree about how they wanted the cleanup to go (and this is what happens when you have too many cooks in the kitchen who want to prove they are each the best). Let the battle games ensue!

At one point, all three women were screaming at people to do different things. Some of the younger employees came up to me, to ask what they should actually be doing because they kept getting different stories. Since I'd been working the events at the museum longer than any of these women had been managing events there, I knew the protocol and where everything went. So, I started telling these other employees what the procedure was, and they started doing it. This apparently pissed off one of the women really badly, and she decided to take her anger out on me by screaming at me from the first floor while I was on the second floor, beginning to walk towards the bridge. I just stopped and stared at her like she had lost her mind. My first reaction was to tell her to stop being a controlling asshole, but I knew that wouldn't get us anywhere, and everybody really just wanted to go home at this point. So, I let her finish her screaming diatribe, and then I calmly turned around and continued walking towards the bridge. I have no idea if she said anything after that, and I really don't care. By then, I knew I was done with Rocky Top, and I never worked another shift for them.

| | |
|---|---|
| ★ | Sometimes, it is beneficial to try to get into a company through multiple different ways, if the first way doesn't work |
| ★ | Being responsible and reliable can get you further in a position than just experience alone |
| ★ | Having a good team to work with is integral to pulling off a larger event |

# Contract Catering
## at the Temple

When I first started catering with Irregardless, my initial mentor was a woman named Diane. She was older than I was but had been doing catering for a while. Our personalities meshed, for the most part, so I paid attention to what she was doing, and she taught me the processes they preferred to use.

However, about a year or so into working with them, things started to go downhill with Diane. She became less reliable, flighty, and started drinking with guests at events. This is a major no-no! Basically, she had some personal stuff going on in her life that was sending her into a tailspin, and it was translating across to her job. So, Diane and Irregardless parted ways.

But she and I remained in touch because I really did like her as a person, even if I was disappointed about the situation. I didn't see her for almost a year, and in that time, she had begun to do some work with a local wood restoration company. This was pretty cool, in my book, because it displayed her diversity. She also had been in contact with one of the local Jewish temples about catering with them. She knew them because her closest friend at Irregardless, Dena, worked at the temple full-time and just moonlighted in the catering world for extra cash.

As Diane started to pick up catering gigs at the temple, she reached out to me, to see if I would be interested in helping her for $100 per event. Why, *yes*, yes, I would!

These gigs were much more sporadic, but the pay was much better and so was the working environment. I helped her set up the room, including tables and place settings, as well as helped set up decorations. Then, once that was done, I would work on helping her with the layout of the food from an aesthetic perspective because she knew this was one of my areas of expertise. But she also knew that I had a background in food, cooking and baking, and that I knew my way around a kitchen and was good with flavor profiles. Because of that knowledge, she had me help her in the kitchen, preparing the food and/or figuring out food choices, also.

She and I really worked well together, so we made a great team. Everything at the temple depended on the season, so the work was certainly sporadic. But I always ended up taking leftover food home, also, so I couldn't complain. Diane and I are still in touch, but I haven't worked an event with her at the temple in almost a year now.

★ Keeping in touch with old co-workers can be beneficial for new job opportunities

★ Everybody runs events differently, so learning to adapt to their individual style is a must

★ Having a more diverse skill set can assist with getting more dynamic job offers

# CBRE
# (Microsoft Account)

During the summer of 2013, an old friend, for the third time, approached me about working with her. I had turned her down the two previous times because I didn't think working at Microsoft would end up being a good fit for me. My thoughts about this came from the fact that I did some temp work with her at Microsoft in the exact position that she wanted me to take a few times in 2011 and 2012. While I enjoyed the atmosphere, the campus was in Durham and would take me almost an hour to commute each time. That was coupled with the fact that, at this point, I had my children about 85% of the time, so I had to find somebody to watch my daughter all day and somebody to take my son to school and pick him up. That was a challenge, needless to say!

But when she approached me for the third time, I was working the few different positions at the Science Museum and catering with Irregardless. What that meant for me was that the money was unstable and unpredictable, so the stable paycheck was the main allure. At least with a stable paycheck, I would know what I was bringing in every month. Plus, she told me they had a great 401(k) matching program, sick time, and vacation time, none of which I had since my Diamond Hill days.

She told me it was time to grow up and be a stable parent, and she was giving me the opportunity to do that. While I disagreed with that assessment, and it means she never really understood me or how I operate, I decided to take it. Plus, they were paying me $32,000 a year, with the potential for some monthly overtime.

I wasn't sure how I was going to make it work because this was the end of July, and school didn't start until the end of August. My daughter would be starting kindergarten, though, so that would help because they would both be in school. This meant I would need to find somebody to keep them in the morning and bring them to the bus stop because I was able to get the YMCA afterschool care at their school for a reduced cost.

My ex-husband and I were also switching to a fifty-fifty schedule once our daughter started school, so we would each have them for one full week and one full week off. We still have the same schedule today, and it really helps with work and trips. This upcoming custody schedule change would help alleviate some of the pressure, also, which is what made me think I could make this successfully work.

My job was really simple and, honestly, bored me to tears. However, I had decided back in the spring that I was going back to grad school to get my Master's of Nutrition degree and had taken the GRE to get accepted. Since my job at Microsoft didn't require much brain cell function from me, and I had a lot of downtime, it meant that I could do some schoolwork for my degree.

I hate to tell you that I can't remember the actual title of the position anymore, but I was basically the front desk secretary. I would get there at 8:00 a.m.—at least that was when I was supposed to be there—and unlock the doors to both suites. Then, I would turn on all of the lights, start the giant coffee maker, turn my computer on, and take the phones off of night mode. Then, I would sit there and wait for employees to come in or see if I had any emails to respond to.

The list of my actual duties, although not necessarily done every day, were:

- Take pictures of new employees for their security badges and hand them out when they came in
- Send out anything via FedEx that was required
- Fix the printers when they jammed up, as well as refill the paper and ink
- Book, setup, and break down conferences for the conference rooms
- Order lunches and drinks for the conferences
- Make sure the A/V in the conference rooms was working
- Troubleshoot the A/V and/or call tech to help me if I couldn't figure it out
- Check the lamps and change them when need be in each conference room
- Clean the white boards, tables, and desks in each conference room with sanitizing wipes
- Clean the microwaves and refrigerators in the kitchens of each suite
- Restock the soda coolers, tea, and coffee in each suite (there were four)
- Take inventory of the above-mentioned products
- Adjust the spreadsheet for Canteen and send it to my supervisor for her approval before I placed the soda/tea/coffee order
- Check in the Canteen order when it showed up weekly and then distribute it to each suite
- Check the mail and distribute it to the correct office
- Answer the phones and transfer them to the correct person

Since I was working on my master's, I asked if I could help set up a Wellness division for the East Coast. My big boss loved the idea and told me she would get it in the works. In my mind, this was something I loved and could work on during the times of severe boredom. But apparently, she was thinking this would be a different position entirely, and after months of hearing nothing back, even though I inquired regularly, I was told that it just wasn't in the budget. You have seriously got to be kidding me!

I remember there were times, especially on Fridays, that it was a ghost town, but I still had to be there. During those times, I would entertain myself by running up and down the stairs (because we had three suites on the first floor and one on the second) or running wind sprints down the hall on the second floor. I realize it sounds stupid, but I was trying to keep myself from going insane. I was dying of boredom. I could feel my brain cells withering up, and it was killing me!

The bigger issue ended up being my getting to work on time and being able to pick my kids up from afterschool care on time. Even though my very kind neighbor had agreed to watch my kids in the morning and take them to the bus stop, there had been a few hiccups with the bus not showing up at all a few times. She had a full-time job, so that was a problem for her; plus she didn't have any car seats.

Not only that but the traffic was a nightmare! It was so unpredictable that it could take me anywhere from thirty minutes to an hour and a half to get there. I'm not sure if you're seeing the problem yet, but for somebody with kids who is relying on the kindness of a neighbor to watch her kids, that is a big issue. The deal was that I would make sure they were ready for school and have them fed before I dropped them off at 7:00 a.m., which I did. But I just didn't make it to work on time every time, and every day, it was stressful for me.

I realize this was a problem for Microsoft, but I simply can't control traffic. Once I figure that out, I will let you know! Their solution was for me to leave at 6:30 a.m. instead, and if I got there early, I could just sit in the parking lot until the exterior doors of the building opened. Yeah, that may have sounded like a good solution to them, but that wasn't going to work for me and my situation, as previously noted. Not only that, but on my way into work one morning, in October that year, somebody decided that he didn't see all of the red lights ahead of him from the stopped traffic and plowed into me at 60 mph, causing a five-car pileup. My car looked like an accordion, and I ended up in the hospital with a concussion.

By this point, my friend, who had wanted me in this position so badly, was constantly ticked off at me. And to a degree, I understood, but what she has never understood was my position as a single parent and living that far away. This was simply just not a good situation for me or my kids. Even with that being the case, I had a very difficult time with the feeling that I was letting her down and potentially ruining our friendship because I couldn't make it work. I know she had good intentions when she brought me on and was hoping that it would strengthen our relationship. Unfortunately, it had the opposite effect. And for that, I will always feel some guilt for the part I played in the demise of our relationship.

The afterschool care only lasted until 6:00 p.m., and if you were late, you had to pay a fee, which I didn't have the money for. Traffic in the afternoons could be just as bad as in the morning, so there were a few times when I was late getting them. The whole time I was driving there, I was extremely stressed out, and that didn't help my state of mind. On top of it, the kids felt like they never got to see me anymore, and up until then, I was technically a stay-at-home mom, so this was a huge adjustment. By the time we got home in the evenings, I was rushing to throw something together for dinner, while they worked on homework, and then it was straight into the bath, books, and bedtime. We had no time to just be with each other, and I missed this the most.

I knew I was done with this position, by this point. I should have listened to my gut because it knew better, but hindsight is definitely 20/20. My friend and I haven't spoken since my last day at Microsoft, at the end of May in 2014, which is extremely sad, especially because her son is my godson.

Once I made the decision to leave, I reached out to my old boss, Albert, in Special Exhibits at the museum, and he told me he would love to have me back. But the caveat was that he really needed me in the box office because I was good with numbers, problem-solving, and customer relations. He agreed to pay me a little bit more, also, but, alone, it still wasn't going to be enough to make ends meet.

During my time with Microsoft, I didn't do as much catering, but I was still with Irregardless and Rocky Top, so I figured I could just pick up more regular shifts with each company. On top of that, I did happen to work a catering event for Rocky Top that was in conjunction with The Umstead Hotel, and while at the event, one of their managers tried to pluck me from Microsoft. I will get to that story next.

★ Always listen to your gut; it is smarter than you!

★ I greatly detest traffic, and it causes me unnecessary stress

★ Working an 8:00 a.m.–5:00 p.m. job is simply not suited for me

★ I require more brain stimulation on a regular basis so I don't try to poke my eyeballs out with the nearest sharp office supply

★ A regular income is helpful for my budget, but spending time with my kids is more important

# The Umstead Hotel and Spa Banquets & IRD

A s mentioned in the Microsoft section, I ran across The Umstead Hotel while I was catering an event for Rocky Top. Matt, the manager I mentioned, and I worked very well together at the event. I met the GM of Banquets (Jose), the Executive Chef (Scott), and the Sous Chef (Tim), also. Please keep in mind that I wasn't looking for another side gig because I had plenty at this point, but I really like The Umstead crew. So I entertained Matt's idea of adding The Umstead as another potential side gig, especially because he told me the hourly rate was better than what Rocky Top was paying me.

Naturally, this piqued my interest, so I filled out an application, as per Matt, and sent it to Jose. He called me a couple of days after I submitted it and asked me to come in for an interview the next week. We worked out the time, and I met him at the hotel. Getting into his office was a very similar experience to when I worked at Disney World, in that they have a completely different hidden entrance for employees and the hallways are below the first floor. Jose and I spoke briefly about the Banquets Department and what his needs were. He was happy to hear that I had bartending experience because they didn't have any female bartenders on staff at the time in that department. He also liked my work ethic, based on what he saw at the event we previously worked together at. He asked me what I was looking for, and I told him it couldn't be anything full-time because I was currently at Microsoft full-time. He asked me if I had a set time schedule I could work, and I told him no, but that I was very communicative and responsive, so I could promise him a schedule a month in advance, and he could schedule me from that. He agreed that was sufficient notice and would fit me in wherever he could.

The pay rate there is different than any other place I have worked. They paid minimum wage as the base pay, but every event would have a different bonus, basically, that would be added on top of the base. For each event, a certain percentage of the BEO (Banquet Event Order) was designated for staffing, and everybody who worked the event, besides managers, would split that evenly by how many hours they worked. It sounded much more complicated than the other catering companies, but it made statistical sense in my brain. I just wasn't sure how that was going to look on paper until I got my first check. The long and short of it is that it usually worked out to be anywhere from $17 - $20 per hour. This was not shabby in the catering world!

The way they worked is there was an employee-only parking lot further away from the hotel, and you had to walk over to the employee-only entrance and put in a code, which was changed monthly, into the security box to gain entrance into the building. Then, you had to go over to Uniforms to get your uniform and then hit the timeclock on the wall and clock in before heading to the locker rooms to change. Each person was fitted for a uniform for their specific department, and we usually each had two so we could switch them out to get washed by laundry, which was awesome because I didn't have to take them home and wash them. This was also like working at Disney World in almost every aspect, including the separate café downstairs, at which the employees could take their breaks and eat. Keep in mind that your clock-in time was what you got paid from, but you had to be in your department and ready to go at your call time, which meant that, in order to change clothes, you had to get there earlier than your expected time.

I can't say I was a huge fan of the uniforms in Banquets because they were suits, which I don't think any woman should have to wear. They were really hot, also, which made running around before, during, and after events extra sweaty.

A lot of the staff in Banquets worked at other hotels, so I seemed to be the odd man out. There were a few full-time staff in Banquets who made good money, but they worked like crazy people. A common denominator I found was that the pay was decent, but they would work you to death if you let them. I didn't have the time to let them work me to death, at this point, but that changed later on.

I really liked the staff I worked with, and they showed me the ropes well, not only for working in a hotel but working up to a five-star standard, since The Umstead is a five-star hotel. There are certain ways things must be done to keep the five-star rating, and I found out we weren't allowed to ask any guests how they were doing, but were just supposed to say, "Hello, Mr. and Mrs. Whatever." We had to be more specific with our line of questioning such as, "Is there anything I may be able to assist you with?" or "Would you care for a drink?" Formality does not really fit my personality, as I am slightly more casual and sarcastic by nature, so this was a really difficult task for me. I can't tell you I succeeded in the formal speech, but I tried, which was all I could really do. Nobody ever complained, though, so I must have pulled it off with some modicum of success.

More often than not, I was a catering bartender, which I really liked. This was more of my natural area because I could be a little bit less formal with the guests. We each got our own bar to stock and roll out, which was great, but those suckers were *heavy* and hard to maneuver. I can tell you that I ran into a wall or two in my time, but it looks like other people did before me, also, so I didn't feel as bad about it.

Bartending was easy but the catering aspect was more intricate than any of the other catering jobs I had worked before. They taught me about synchronized serving which not only looked beautiful but was pretty easy to pull off, as long as you were organized and all on the same page.

I didn't work a ton of events because I just didn't have the time, but once I left Microsoft, I was open to working more events. In steps my good buddy, Matt, who just happened to be the supervisor in IRD (In Room Dining). He had been trying to get me to work in his department with him for months, at this point, but I just couldn't swing it. I finally agreed to let him train me in IRD, even though I had no idea what that even was. The pay scale was similar, and both departments would end up being on the same check. I found out later that a lot of their full-time employees work in multiple departments so they can get overtime on their check, but it doesn't all come out of one department's budget.

The long and short of this story is that, after some time, both departments were utilizing me on a regular basis, and there were times when they fought over where I should be. Banquets argued that they hired me first, but IRD argued that they used me more regularly and had less people in their department, so they should get me. It was actually pretty funny in my opinion. There were a few times when I would work both jobs almost simultaneously because both departments were short staffed. That was *really* hard for me to pull off because both departments have different uniforms.

The gist of IRD depended on whether I was working a morning shift or a night shift. I ended up working more morning shifts because most of the banquets were at night, so that was easier to manage, being scheduled in both departments on the same day. For the morning shift, I would come in and see what room service had been requested during the night and help set up tables with the accoutrements required for the associated food. I would then talk to the MOD, to see what their thoughts were for the day and if there was anything special going on I needed to know about. The next thing I would do was go downstairs to dry storage and restock on anything that we were low on. This was one of my favorite tasks because I am a little bit OCD and like to have everything in an organized manner before I get my ass handed to me. By that, I mean before we got hit with the breakfast and brunch rush and were running around like chickens with our heads cut off. It was actually something people would joke with me about because they said everybody knew when I had been working, since all of the labels all faced the same way and everything was fully stocked. Yep, that would be me—the semi-OCD crazy person!

As soon as food orders started coming up in the window, we would take them and put them on the appropriate IRD table, to bring up to the rooms. If everything was on the table and ready to go at the requested time, we would each roll off with a table—sometimes two or three on extremely busy weekend days—and go to deliver the goods to the guests. This was the part of the day when you really got slammed because there was usually a two- to three-hour period of time when it seemed like everybody and their mother was ordering food. On days when we were short staffed, it was a real marathon, which I liked because I got a good workout in. Sometimes, the guests would tip us, and if they did, we got to keep the tip. Unfortunately, it didn't happen that often, so it was more of a special surprise than something to be expected.

After the breakfast rush, we would restock and reorganize the IRD area of the kitchen for lunch. A few people would start walking the halls to see if any guests had pushed their tables out to be cleared. If so, they would roll them to the employee elevator area, behind a set of doors that just looks like another room door, and clear off all of the debris so the only thing they were bringing down were scraped dishes. Sometimes, we would have six or seven tables in these small landings we were trying to clear at once, so it could get hairy. Once the tables were cleared, we had to bring them downstairs to the dish pit and put the dirty dishes in the appropriate location, then clear the linens off the table and start resetting it.

Each day, one person had to work the minibar, and I found that this was something I really liked to do, so it got handed off to me a lot. The person handling the minibar would have to print off the sheet of rooms that were occupied the night before so we could check each minibar for items taken and charge the guest accordingly. There was a minibar cart in the downstairs area that we had to make sure was fully stocked prior to starting the rounds because that is what we refilled the minibars with. Next to each room, we either marked it off if nothing was taken, or we put down what was replenished so we could add up the charges back in the IRD office.

I enjoyed this because I was left to my own devices and it was quiet.

Plus, I like math and finding fun surprises that people either left in their refrigerators or tried to sneak in as replacements for something they obviously took.

The bonus for the person doing the minibar was that they would get a percentage of the charges for the day added to their regular pay, although they usually ended up staying later than everybody else on the morning shift. Sometimes, this worked out well for me, but other times, it was a struggle if I had to work in Banquets or another catering job.

As for the night-shift routine, the first person in would usually work on amenities. At first, I had no idea what the heck they were talking about, but after they trained me, it was pretty easy. Guests who were celebrating special events, or were just special guests for one reason or another, would get an amenity in their room, waiting for them upon check-in. A lot of times, this was chocolate-dipped strawberries or macaroons served with either bottled water or wine, but sometimes, it was a more complicated charcuterie plate or fruit display. It really all just depended on the occasion and whether or not it was given to them as a gift from hospitality or whether they paid for the amenity. Overall, it was pretty easy, though. The person would get the amenity list, pull all of the amenities and accompaniments, and deliver them to the appropriate rooms. Easy peasy.

If you were working on amenities, you were walking the halls to make sure there weren't any rogue tables in the hallways because that was a no-no. Then, you would make sure there were enough linens for all of the tables and ensure they were dressed and ready for the dinner rush.

I wasn't as big of a fan of the dinner shift because there was a lot more lag time, and to fill it, all we really worked on was polishing silverware and glassware. I really disliked that because it killed my hands!

And this was a place where you didn't ever want to be caught standing around with nothing to do—not that I enjoy that anyway. I would always rather be busy, so the morning shift was my preference.

But, whenever I did work the night shift, I found plenty of things to do. One of the big tasks I undertook at night was reorganizing all of the glassware. We had a problem with so much glassware and not enough space to store it. So it could be found all over the place. I worked with the head of the dishwashing department to get this organized. Since the dishwashers were the ones replacing the racks of glasses, sometimes they weren't all put back in the correct racks. Other times, the glasses weren't returned to the dish pit by Banquets or IRD in full racks of the correct glasses. So, by working together, we figured out a better place to store all of them, labeled the floor for each type of glass, and regularly worked with our departments to make sure they were putting everything where it belonged. While this wasn't a brain stimulating activity, it gave me something useful to do; plus, I got to use my love of organization and labels. Overall, it worked out pretty well and made things much easier for all three departments.

Matt ended up leaving the department right after he trained me. He went into the Reservations Department, so we got a new supervisor, Ben. Ben was a cool guy, but he was much younger than me and wet behind the ears. We talked a lot and became work friends, which is the same with another one of my IRD co-workers, Jeannette. At first, she worked more of the nightshifts, but as time went on, and her life situation changed, she started working more of the morning shifts with me. Ben liked working with me, so he put me on the schedule a lot. So much so, that I began working over forty hours a week just at The Umstead alone.

I knew this job wouldn't be forever, though, because I wasn't going to school to get my master's to do something that didn't require it. So, right after I graduated in December of 2015, I stopped working for The Umstead. My last shift was on Christmas Eve, although I remained on their employee list until the next summer. I just wasn't able to give them any shifts because I was too busy with other endeavors. I don't believe there were any hard feelings, as it was just one of those jobs that ran its course.

44

**What I Learned**

★ Sometimes, being in the right place at the right time does pay off

★ Working in a five-star hotel is a completely different animal

★ You should tip your in-room-dining servers, just like everybody else

★ Flexibility and mobility is something that works well for me

★ Finding extra things to do during slow times can really help the business as a whole, even if it seems like a mundane task

# THE ROOF IS
# ON FIRE

# North Carolina Museum of Natural Sciences (Box Office)

hen I made the decision that I needed to get out of Microsoft, I reached out to my old boss at the Science Museum, as previously mentioned. Albert told me he would be really happy to have me back because they were short staffed. However, the caveat would be that he needed me downstairs in the box office instead of upstairs in the Special Exhibit hall. He offered me a dollar more an hour, also, so that helped. Even though, that only brought me up to $11 an hour which was certainly not great.

That meant I was leaving a job that had been paying me approximately $15.38 per hour to take one that was paying me over $4 less an hour! Oh, yeah, I was using my brain on this one. But (and there is always a "but" in my book) the Science Museum gave me the flexibility that my life required. And at this point in my life, I have come to realize that is more important to me than the hourly rate.

The other aspect to this change was that I would be able to go back to working for my mother at her company, Bell & Associates, one day a week. She was grateful to have me back because she hadn't really been doing her books while I was at Microsoft, and by the time I came back, they were a HOT MESS! I told her she wasn't allowed to touch her books ever again. Of course, that was an exaggeration, but the point was there.

So now, we are at the Science Museum four days a week, my mother's one day a week, working for Irregardless and Rocky Top whenever events popped up that I could work, and working nights and weekends at The Umstead Hotel. Overall, I ended up making more money doing this than I did at Microsoft, but it took some organization and planning. My calendar looked like a rainbow threw up on it, but I was perfectly fine with that. Because it meant, the weeks I had my kids, I could work while they were in school, and that was about it. I could also get more schoolwork done on those weeks. The weeks I didn't have my kids, I worked my butt off and got little to no sleep. I also didn't have to ask permission to take a day off or go on vacation because I gave everybody my availability ahead of time, so they never knew if I was working for somebody else or not. And it didn't really matter to them, anyway. This was another big driving factor for me because I greatly detested having to turn in a vacation request form and then waiting around to see if it was approved or denied. For me, that has always been a bit ridiculous, and I loved that I didn't have to engage in that kind of behavior anymore. Ultimately, I was the master of my own schedule and was willing to work myself to death to keep my freedom.

But back to the box office job, now! One of the biggest perks of the museum was that I could come in as soon as my kids got on the bus and leave to go pick them up, and nobody ever gave me any grief. I could also walk from home on the days I didn't have the kids, as long as I didn't have to go directly to another job. And it was a nice slightly-over-one-mile walk, so I enjoyed that aspect. I was also able to bring my kids with me to work a few times when they were out of school.

They were allowed to go into the theater and watch the 3D movies, wander the museum, hang out in the Special Exhibit hall and help out (although that didn't happen but more than once, in my recollection), or hang out with me, as well, in the box office and read or draw. This was a huge perk for me because it took a lot of the stress off surrounding what to do with my kids when they were out of school and I needed to work. I appreciate the museum for that privilege.

When I first came back, they had to train me on the box office computers, regarding the programs and the process for tickets. The system they were using was pretty darn easy to grasp, so it didn't take me too long to get it. Figuring out how to unjam the printers was a whole different story, though, as those things were dinosaurs! Sometimes, what was really needed was a hard reset to get them functional again. Of course, that usually happened when we had a line out the door. Good old Murphy's Law strikes again!

Because Albert believed in my math skills, he had me work on the monthly timecards, so he could process them for payment. The timecards we used were fairly antiquated, as well, so that made things more interesting. We would clock in with this large timecard, but it just stamped the in and out time, and never did any math, as to how long you were working. Not only that, but each day, we had to clock out for lunch, also, so there would be four stamps on each day worked. Therefore, he had me work on adding up the correct time each person worked on each day so that, when I handed him the timecards towards the end of the month, the math was already done for him, and he could just enter the numbers into his system. This was not very difficult to do, but it was time consuming, so I understood his plight. It gave me something to do to kill time, though, so I was happy to help.

The other thing we worked on in the box office was other small projects for Albert. Sometimes, I would create spreadsheets for him or Word docs for a project he needed for something else. I really liked these because I love to create Word docs and Excel spreadsheets. I realize I am a total nerd when I say this, but it is true!

Also, at least once a month, but sometimes more often, the Friends of the Museum Department upstairs would send down a box of membership information for me to fold and stuff. This was another project that didn't take any brainpower but helped kill some time during the times we were slow. In case you haven't noticed by now, I don't like to be bored, and I don't like to sit on anybody's clock not doing anything. It doesn't make me feel good, and it doesn't make me feel like they are getting the most out of what they are paying me, even if it is only $11 an hour.

But my favorite special project of all was working on selling memberships. You see, the museum is free to get into, but the movies and special exhibits are paid attractions. If you become a member of the museum, you get in at a reduced cost or completely free, depending upon the exhibit. The museum is part of a network called ASTC (Association of Science and Technology Centers) and is similar to the AZA (Association of Zoos and Aquariums). Some centers have both accreditations, and if that is the case, your membership will get you into any of the aforementioned, which is completely awesome! This science museum has applied for their AZA, but it still hasn't been granted.

Overall, if you become a member, you get into the special exhibits for free and into the movies for $2 per person. The museum also hosts certain events that are for members only. And to top it off, you are able to get into over 300 museums nationwide for free with your membership. Believe me when I tell you that my children and I have used that membership like it is a magic ticket whenever we go on a vacation. It has saved me a ton of money over the years, and it only cost me $70 for the year to purchase it. Well, actually, at the time, mine was free because it was a perk of being an employee, but you get my drift.

Now that you've heard what it is, you can see how passionate I became about selling memberships. As I previously mentioned, the museum is run partially by government funds and partially as a non-profit. Well, the Friends of the Museum Department I told you about earlier is the non-profit side of the museum, and memberships are a big part of what keeps the museum afloat. So, as a side note, since that side is non-profit, when you purchase a museum membership, it's considered a tax write-off, depending upon how you do your taxes. Extra bonus!

I started talking to each guest about memberships when they asked for tickets, and if they weren't members, I tried to quickly explain the benefits. At first, I was selling one or two a day sometimes, but that all depended on the traffic and where the guests were from. You see, ASTC has a passport program which states that you need to purchase a membership closest to where you live. This is because the passport program has a ninety-mile clause, where they don't have to honor reciprocal agreements with other museums within ninety miles. The reason for this is because, if they didn't do that, everybody would find the cheapest museum membership in the country and purchase it but then use the membership at their much more expensive, but closer-to-home, museums. That wouldn't work out well for most museums, hence the clause. It makes complete sense to me, but that meant I didn't want people who lived somewhere else to purchase our membership and screw over their local museum; plus, then they wouldn't be able to use the membership at their local museum. Because the museum will look at your address, and if you live in the same area as the museum but are using a membership from somewhere else, they have the right to not grant you entry. Basically, the clause is to keep people honest, and I refused to sell a bill of goods to somebody who might not serve them well in the long run, just to get a sale.

Overall, I think my best record ended up being twenty-two memberships in one day, and I was pretty darn happy with that! I started spending more time training other employees about the memberships and what to say to guests. Albert had me work on a training program and train the employees in the Special Exhibit hall to discuss memberships, as well as the crew in the box office. They told me they hadn't had anybody really working on museum membership sales in quite a while, and they were grateful that I took an interest in it. I was happy to help, and I really liked talking to guests about the ASTC membership because I wholeheartedly believed in it, and I still do today.

At one point, I did ask for a raise, and Albert was able to give me a dollar more an hour, but that was the max they could do at the time. Beggars can't be choosers, so I took it. We were also giving away some swag during the holiday season for guests that purchased memberships. There was this olive-green backpack with Acrocanthosaurus (Acro was our museum mascot because we had a huge one on display on the third floor) on it that I really wanted. I asked them how much it costs, and it was more than I could afford at the moment, especially for a backpack. So I asked Albert if he would consider it to be a gift if I sold a certain amount of memberships. He talked to the Friends of the Museum because, essentially, it belonged to them, and they agreed.

The other thing I worked out with Albert was that, if we, as a staff, could hit a certain number of memberships sold by the end of the year, then he would throw us all a party with some swag giveaways. He liked this idea because it was positive motivation, and the staff pretty much all seemed to be on board with the new influx of energy surrounding selling memberships. He told the staff there would be a party with prizes if we all reached the goal, together as a team, so that seemed to light a fire under some butts.

Overall, we reached our goals, and some of us even got into a friendly contest, regarding who could sell the most in a day. I won a lot, on the days I was there, but there were definitely some other front runners in the mix, now. Sam and Nick are the main two that come to mind, as they were knowledgeable and very personable, so it made selling memberships pretty easy for them once they put their minds to it.

Eventually, I did end up getting my Acro backpack, and I loved it, and Albert did throw the party. However, he chose to throw the party on a day when I couldn't come, even after we all gave him our availability. Needless to say, I was a bit ticked off because the whole idea came from me in the first place. Scottie, his right-hand lady, said they would buy me some gluten-free pizza for lunch the next time I worked, but they never did. And since I wasn't there, I didn't get to partake in the choosing of the prizes, so they brought me back a turtle garden stake. While it was nice in theory, I didn't garden. Hell, I was sleeping maybe four hours a night because I worked so much, so I never saw my house!

This whole thing left a bad taste in my mouth. Since I had begun to cut my hours down at the museum to only three days a week because I was working more at The Umstead, it started to make sense in my brain to begin to phase myself out of the box office. After the issue with the memberships, I changed my schedule to only work two days a week and picked up another day in IRD at The Umstead because they paid more. Not too long after that, I told Albert I wasn't going to work regularly in the box office anymore but that he could keep me on call if they were short-staffed. He said he understood I had to go where I could make more money, but he was sad to see me go. Although, he still sees me when I'm back working as a contractor, but it isn't the same.

**45**

**What I Learned**

★ Never burning bridges is important because you never know if you might need that person or that job again

★ I like taking on new projects and learning new skills

★ I enjoy creating training programs and implementing them

★ I am a huge nerd for Word docs and Excel spreadsheets!

# Ascenda Medical

One of my good friends just happened to own her own business in the medical industry. She knew I worked at TriE for years and had experience in the medical industry, so she offered me a contract position with her, working on some random projects. She offered to pay me $30 an hour, which she said was low, based on my skill set, but it was all she could offer at the time. I was not balking at that amount, based on what I had been getting paid, so, of course, I said yes.

Since she was working with clients in the medical field, she had to sign NDA's (Non-Disclosure Agreement) which meant I also had to sign them. While at TriE, I had experience with this before, so it wasn't considered an unusual practice, in my opinion. She just wanted to make sure it wasn't going to be an issue before we proceeded with the first project, which I appreciate.

We didn't actually end up working together on a lot of projects because she prefers to keep enough work to keep her busy but isn't trying to build an empire, which I not only understand but respect. So in the six or nine months we did work together, I believe I worked on three to four different projects for her. We would have a meeting at the beginning of a project, to go over the scope of the work needed. A lot of what she was having me do was research and compile data, which is something I really like (see the above note about my love of spreadsheets!).

The last project I worked on for her was during an online video meeting she was hosting, and she needed me to take copious notes so she had something to reference for her clients afterwards. This was a pretty interesting call, but it was hard for me to really get the gist of it because I was so busy writing down the key points.

I enjoyed working with her, overall, because we work well together. We have a similar work ethic, although I certainly work harder than she does. But then, she works smarter than I do. She is a good person to collaborate with and gives good feedback on projects, which is a skill lacking in a lot of people. So I can appreciate the time we spent together on projects, although it was short lived.

★ Working with a like-minded friend can be very rewarding

★ You never know who is going to offer you a job

★ It is nice, and surprising, when somebody actually recognizes your worth and is willing to pay you accordingly

★ I am tired of not being paid appropriately for my skill level

# Private Catering

During the summer of 2014, a co-worker of mine at the Science Museum, Bill, called me up to see if I would be willing to cater a private event he was having at his house for some of the staff. I asked him what it entailed, and he told me he bought all of the food but that he needed somebody to set up everything, prep, put the food out, replenish, take care of taking guests' plates, and cleaning up. I told him that would be easy compared to what I had been doing in catering already, especially since he only expected it to be around forty guests. I asked him about the compensation, and he said he had budgeted $100 to pay me. I told him that would be fine and that I would be there.

The day of the event, I showed up around 4:00 p.m. to start setting up tables, a self-serve bar area, and start prepping fruit and veggie trays in the garage. All I really had to do was set out the food options, display them nicely, and in the most efficient way possible, streamline traffic under the tent. Then, I had to clear plates, and I would go around and ask if anybody wanted their drinks refilled. I even brought some people beers in the pool area. They loved that! Then, I began to clean up once people started leaving. Most of the items were disposable, but since it was primarily a potluck, there were some guests' dishes I needed to wash in the kitchen.

The first year, I did this by myself. But the second year, he asked if I could bring help because he was going to have more people and more food. I invited one of my co-workers from The Umstead, Matthew, to assist me. We each got $100 for that event, which neither one of us argued about. The third and last year I did it, I told him I wasn't really doing catering anymore but that I'd be willing to if he was willing to up his budget. I then told him I would bring my chef partner, Bryan, to assist but that he would have to pay us $250 total. He wasn't that happy about it, but he agreed, and he also agreed to let Bryan run the grill so he could spend more time mingling. That event went over without a hitch, and Bill said he was very excited about how well the fish came out that Bryan cooked; plus, it took more pressure off of him so he could just enjoy the party. We had a great time doing it for him, but I think our prices were too high, so he has been doing it himself again.

Another odd private catering gig I got was through people at the temple where I had done work for Diane. I'm not sure why they didn't ask her to cater their private event, but they didn't. I had no idea who these people were, but they called me out of the blue and told me some people at the temple had mentioned me and that I was good and would do private in-home catering. I told them I would cater the event but that my rate was $100, unless it was an all-day event, for which the rate would be higher. This was a mother and daughter duo who were having back-to-back parties, one night after the other, for a Jewish holiday I know nothing about. Putting that aside, all they needed me to do was pretty much the same thing I did for Bill, but it was inside, in air conditioning. Sold! The first two events were in the spring of 2015, and the mother called me again in the fall of 2015 to ask me if I would work another one for her. So I worked a total of three events for them that year but then didn't hear from them again until earlier this year, 2018, to see if I would be willing to cater the same event. I told her, unfortunately, I was out of the game now and just didn't have the time to do it, plus we had all of the kids that weekend. But I thanked her for keeping me in mind and told her I was sure she would find somebody great.

Bryan and I have also run a few private catering events at people's houses where we provided the food. There have been less than a handful of them, but all of them have been referred to us from friends or former clients or guests. For these events, we work out the menu ahead of time and customize it for their wants and needs. Two of the times, we have done mini classes, where we show them how we are making each course and serve it with either a crafted cocktail or a wine. The other times we have done this, we have not done it classroom style but rather served the guests in different areas of the house for each different course. These courses all had custom alcoholic pairings, as well, and those were always a big hit. We love doing this kind of stuff because we work so well together as a team and are very creative with our food and beverage choices. This type of work really just makes us both light up and highlights our natural skills for the world to see.

**47**

**What I Learned**

★ I really enjoy catering in-home private events for cash

★ Creating customized menus with custom pairings is a real passion of mine

★ Working events with Bryan is one of my favorite things to do for which I get paid

★ Bryan and I work better together than almost anyone else I have ever worked with

★ Coming up with an appropriate presentation with whatever people happen to have in their kitchen can be a challenge, but one that I gladly accept

# North Carolina Museum
# of Natural Sciences
# (Living Collections Internship)

When I was working at the box office, at the Science Museum, I was working concurrently on my Master's of Nutrition degree from NC State University. This is only important because, after I'd completed my first semester, the dean informed me I would have to engage in an internship. Now this was the first I had heard of this, and he and I had met twice before I ever enrolled in the program, to go over the details. Needless to say, I was kind of peeved because I didn't know how I was going to have time for an internship or where I was going to get one. Dr. Allen (the dean) told me that any of the labs there in the program would be happy to have me. While that was all great and wonderful, my schedule simply wouldn't allow for that because all of the labs required that you were on campus and in the lab. Even though I could ride my bike to campus, I was a Distance Ed student because of my jobs and my kids. I simply just couldn't be in the physical classes on a weekly basis, nor could I be in a lab. But if that wasn't enough, just wait because here is the kicker!

He also told me he had a rule regarding internships. If your major was Animal Nutrition, you had to do an internship in Human Nutrition, and if your major was Human Nutrition, you had to do an internship in

Animal Nutrition. This rule was implemented to give you the full spectrum of nutrition and how it affects different species. While I appreciated the diversity, I was at a loss for what I was going to do and how I was going to do it. He told me I had about a month to figure it out and submit the signed proposal to him. Oh, yeah, no pressure there!

So I was racking my brain, trying to figure out what to do, when it hit me the next day while I was sitting in the box office. I just happened to see one of the curators for Living Collections walk by and thought about the huge collection of live animals we have. I wondered if they had ever had anybody take a look at the diets of the animals to ensure they were feeding them the best foods for their systems, for overall long-term health, wellness, and survival. So I called him over and asked if I could speak with him for a minute about something. Adrian was interested to hear my proposal and told me it was a possibility they could use my expertise, since they had a few species that had continual tumors and another one that had a Vitamin C issue.

He asked me to send him the form and my proposal so he could take a look at it and sign off on it. We discussed the details a bit further in the following weeks, but the crux of it is that I could do all of the research from home and submit the final findings to him, to make the dietary changes necessary. I would have to do this one species at a time (there were four in all) so his volunteer staff could implement the changes in time for us to see if there were any positive results. This all sounded great to me because it meant I didn't have to be in a lab and that I could work on the research in the wee hours of the morning, if need be.

I began my internship in January of 2015, and it ended in May of 2015. However, I didn't have to present my findings until my final semester, which was the fall of 2015, so I presented it in October 2015.

This was the abstract I presented for my Senior Presentation:

## *The Effects of Dietary Analysis on Lesser Studied Captive Species*
### Shanah Bell

Abstract Body:

The North Carolina Museum of Natural Sciences has had ongoing issues with certain species in their living collections having proclivities for tumor growth and a high propensity for early death. The four predominant species for these inclinations were the *Flying Squirrel, Hedgehog, Guinea Pig, and the Short-Tailed Opossum*. I was asked to analyze the current diet they were being fed and create a dietary plan of action for each one based on my research. The Living Collections Department's goal was to not only increase their life span in captivity and increase the energy level of each species but also to get them excited about their new diets, which could enhance enrichment for these species. Based on the information I was given, they had multiple concerns with the Flying Squirrel's current diet. The species was not interested in eating its core pellet diet at all, and due to that fact, had all of the aforementioned issues. This species required a complete redesign of the diet, in order to ensure their survival. Their concern regarding the Hedgehog's diet revolved mainly around the fact that they believed they were getting too much soy in their predominately pellet diet. This species also required a complete overhaul. The main concern with the Guinea Pig was more specific in that they had suspicions they were not getting enough Vitamin C, and it was affecting their health and energy levels in a negative manner. As for the Short-Tailed Opossum, they had recently lost the last one in their collection at a fairly early age and, therefore, required a complete overhaul of the diet so that, when they were able to procure more of these species, they would have an action plan with which to proceed. They just received two new members of this species last week and are working on incorporating the new diet. Understanding what changes needed to be made for each species—seeing as they are unique and have not been widely studied—to ensure long-term survival and well-being in a captive environment not only benefits the animals and the handlers but the museum and all of the guests who encounter them.

The following are the protocols I recommended and that were implemented by Adrian and his staff for each of the four aforementioned species:

## FLYING SQUIRREL (*Glaucomys* Volans)
Dietary Changes Suggested by Shanah Bell

★ **40% of their diet from various fruits**
- Oranges
- Apples
- Pears
- Peaches
- Plums
- Berries
- Grapes

★ **40% of their diet from various nuts**
- Acorns (extremely easy to find, just walk outside the museum)
- Pumpkin Seeds

- Pine Nuts
- Walnuts
- Hickory Nuts
- Sunflower Seeds
- Pecans (moderately as a treat)

★ **20% of their diet from other various sources including protein, vegetables, and fungi**
- Mealworms (make sure these are dusted with calcium supplement because they are extremely high in phosphorus)
- Truffles/Mushrooms
- Bark/Leaves/Stems (Sugar Maple seems to be their favorite)
- Eggs (Hardboiled)
- Dead mice/voles
- Insects
- Vegetables (Dill Weed, Dandelion Greens, Lettuce, Parsley, Kale, Spinach, Cabbage, Watercress, Chicory Greens, Mustard Greens, Beet Greens)

★ **Calcium supplement options (Calcium to Phosphorus level should stay around 2:1)**
- Oranges (start out with 1-2 slices, twice a week) Age and size dependant
- Rep-Cal Calcium with Vitamin D3 (1/2 Tablespoon per pound of food mixed with fruits or veggies)

★ **If you choose not to give a whole foods diet as listed above, due to the inability to find necessary foods all year or due to budget restrictions, give the following instead:**

- Exotic Nutrition Squirrel Diet with Fruit Pellets (start out with ½ a cup to see how much they care to eat in a day because this species is not known to overeat)
- Supplement with aforementioned nut selection and mealworms
- Rep-Cal Calcium with Vitamin D3 (1/2 Tablespoon per pound of food mixed with food pellets)

---

## HEDGEHOG (*Erinaceus* Europaeus)
Dietary Changes Suggested by Shanah Bell
February 23, 2015

★ **Bulk of their diet from dry cat food (-50% protein/15-20% fat)**
- Wellness Complete Health "Adult Health"
- Kirkland Adult Stages
- Simply Nourish Adult Chicken and Rice

★ **20% of their diet from protein**
- Cooked Chicken
- Cooked Turkey
- Cooked Lamb
- Hardboiled Eggs

★ **15% of their diet from fiber (chitin main source)**
- Centipedes (2-4 daily)
- Millipedes (2-4 daily)
- Waxworms (6-10 daily)
- Mealworms (high phosphorus content, so limit these to smaller portions due to phosphorus/calcium balance required)
- Crickets (1-2 daily)

- Grape Nuts
- Benefiber
- Baby Oatmeal

★ **5%–15% of their diet from dietary fat**
- Dry Cat Foods
- Meat
- Insects
- Eggs

★ **Taurine supplement options (acts as Beta Carotene and necessary for proper quilling)**
- Dry Cat Food
- Eggs
- Chicken
- Tomatoes
- Sweet Potatoes

★ Choline supplement options (to prevent fatty acid deposits in the liver)
- Meat
- Liver
- Lentils
- Cauliflower
- Cabbage

★ **Chromium supplement options (reduces fatty liver disease)**
- Whole grains cooked in chicken broth (whole grain rice and chicken)
- Peas (high phosphorus content though so limit it due to phosphorus/calcium balance needed)
- Corn

I would suggest feeding a dry cat food (one of the ones listed above) as the main source of nutrients required. Follow this with an insect supplementation daily for chitin required for proper fiber requirements and nutrient breakdown. On top of this, I would regularly add in cooked whole-grain rice in chicken broth with a meat source or hardboiled eggs to make sure they are getting enough Chromium and Choline. If you would like to add in any of the above listed fruits and vegetables, I would do so sparingly, seeing as the research has been inconclusive thus far, regarding their proper breakdown of cellulose.

---

## GUINEA PIG (Cavia Porcellus)
Dietary Changes Suggested by Shanah Bell
March 9, 2015

★ Vitamin C
- Rinsed off greens and/or grasses 1-2 times daily
- Kale 1/3 cup
- Parsley 1/3 cup
- Broccoli stalks and leaves 2 Tbsp
- Dandelion Greens 1/3 – 1/2 cup
- Mustard Greens 1/2 – 3/4 cup
- Spinach 1 cup
- Kohlrabi 1/2 cup
- Romaine 8 Outer Leaves (however because this is particularly lower in Vitamin C content I would suggest giving fewer leaves and mixing it with other greens higher in Vitamin C content such as Kale and Dandelion Greens)

★ **Other colorful vegetables 1-2 times daily**
- Red Bell Pepper 2 Tbsp
- Broccoli 1/3 cup
- Cauliflower 4 Flowerets
- Green Bell Pepper 4 Tbsp
- Cherry Tomatoes 1/3 – 1/2 cup
- Carrots 2 Medium Sized

★ **Fruit 2-3 times a week (depending on the sugar content of the fruit)**
- Guava 1 Tbsp
- Strawberries 2 ½ average berries
- Kiwi 2 ½ Tbsp
- Papaya 1/3 cup
- Orange 1/4 – 1/2 of one
- Cantaloupe 1/4 -1/2 cup
- Pineapple 1/3 cup

If the animal is in need of quick Vitamin C, due to illness or pregnancy, I would suggest the Rugby's Vitamin C Liquid supplement in a 25mg dosage once per day until their situation is stabilized enough to put them back on Vitamin C rich foods instead.

---

## SHORT TAILED OPOSSUM (Monodelphis Domestica)

Dietary Changes Suggested by Shanah Bell

April 21, 2015

★ Bulk of their diet from dry opossum, hedgehog, insectivore and/or cat food (30+% protein/9-13% fat/5% fiber)

- Mazuri Insectivore Diet mixed with Wild Rocky Mountain Cat Food
- Exotic Nutrition Opossum Food
- Spike's Delight Hedgehog Food
- Brisky's Short Tail Possum Feed
- Nebraska Feline Diet

★ Supplementation daily with a variety of insects (can dust with calcium powder, prior to feeding, if animal seems deficient)
- Mealworms
- Crickets
- Super Worms
- Waxworms
- Grasshoppers
- Small Earth Worms

★ Daily supplementation with a variety of fruits and vegetables (cut down to bite sized pieces)
- Grapes
- Apples
- Banana
- Pears
- Papaya
- Blueberries
- Raspberries
- Sweet Potatoes
- Peas
- Baby Food

★ **Supplementation with other sources of Protein**
- Tuna
- Hard-Boiled Egg
- Scrambled Egg
- Pinkie Mice
- Mazuri Primate Biscuit
- Cooked, Unseasoned Chicken and/or Human Grade Meat
- Canned Cat Food

Overall, he said all of the species thrived from the changes I suggested and they implemented. In fact, the flying squirrel loved the enrichment I suggested so much they basically begged for it every day. They no longer had an issue getting them to eat, and they were thriving. The guinea pigs lost weight and had shinier coats and more energy. The hedgehogs lost weight and weren't losing their quills, and when they got the new short-tailed opossums in, they did splendidly well with the recommended diet.

The only issue we ran across was fighting against genetics. Apparently, there is not a huge wild population of short-tailed opossums, so most museums get them from the few breeders that are out there. This means there is a lot of cross-breeding and not much genetic diversity. So, unfortunately, the two new short-tailed opossums died after about a year, which he claims is no doing of mine. He said there is just only so much we can do when we're dealing with genetic defects. And he is correct in that I can only do so much with diet, but I was certainly hoping for better results with that species because they are harder to find. From my knowledge, after those two died, they said they would no longer be getting any more in because they just have too many health problems. Which is too bad because they are super cute!

In the end, I was able to pull off my internship, and my dean gave me an A on the project and the presentation. He said it was very well-planned and executed, and he was very interested to hear the results. Adrian and I have discussed publishing these results in a scientific paper but have yet to do so because of our conflicting busy schedules. It may come down to me writing the paper and sending it to him to edit it and then put his name on it. But for right now, it is what it is, and I learned a lot. I will always be grateful for the experience because I really feel for animals as a whole, but especially in captivity. I only want the best for them, and it hurts me to see a lot of what is done, with regard to how animals are typically fed, is actually hurting them instead. This is something I would really like to have a bigger impact on to create more widespread change. After all, animals only want the same things we want, and it makes me feel empathetic towards them when we aren't giving them that when the knowledge is at our disposal. How would you feel if it were you?

**48**

**What I Learned**

★ Sometimes, the solution is right under my nose

★ If no opportunity to problem-solve is clear, create the solution

★ Animals have completely different systems than humans do and require different nutrients to make them operate properly

★ It's a mistake of zoos and museums to feed live animals a human created diet and expect them to live long, healthy lives

★ I love what the museum does for their animals and how much they care about them and their overall well-being

# Adaptive Nourishment, LLC

As I was finishing my master's, I had a class that required we create a project for our proposed business idea, with our business name. This was supposed to be a pretend business, but I knew I was going to be starting my own business once I graduated, so I figured this would be a good opportunity to do it.

I was working on the idea for the food video and was having a difficult time coming up with the name. I knew I wanted it to be something about adapting, since that is a skill I have used my entire life, realizing every change in life is about adapting in some way. A good friend of mine, Tayett, helped me brainstorm some ideas with different words I was floating around and came up with Adaptive Nourishment, LLC. I liked how it sounded together, and it reflected the message I was trying to convey. The next step was for me to check and make sure nobody else in this state had the name, which they didn't, but I also wanted to be sure nobody else in another state had it, either. The name doesn't seem to exist anywhere else that I could find, so I was sold. I registered my business with the SOS (Secretary of State) in November 2015.

Now that I had a name, I had to create the project, which I did with the help of a couple of close friends who were willing to work for food. The video was showing how to make a low-cost, nutrient-dense meal that tastes good in a very efficient manner and is geared more towards certain ethnicities that are on food stamps or SNAP. Since a fairly decent portion of the SNAP recipients in this State are not of American origins, they usually have more ethnic diets. These dietary preferences don't usually work well with the advice given by SNAP for what to eat, so a lot of times, they will just resort to purchasing more prepackaged food instead. By creating this video, I was trying to reach that specific majority that can easily get overlooked with these programs.

Here is a link to the YouTube video, in case you get interested and want to check out the final product:

https://www.youtube.com/watch?v=N_R9itZVUeM

After I graduated in December 2015, my goal was to get my business off the ground with clients and write a blog on my website. I can tell you that plan got derailed by another job opportunity, but it eventually happened. Although it took me until the spring of 2017 to eventually start getting some smaller health clients, I was finally able to get it launched.

Of course, with every business, you may start with one idea of how you think it's going to go but then change course throughout time. That is exactly what happened here. I have found that my biggest struggle in life is getting people to understand how diverse I am, and that I am adaptable to pretty much any situation. Most people I've run across don't think that way and can't switch tasks or topics quickly and seamlessly. That is a superpower of mine. But since people don't usually think this way, they don't know where to put me. A better way of saying this is that they don't know which box to put me into (and I greatly detest boxes, in case you couldn't already tell), so they don't put me in any.

I can assist with any and all health issues, due to my life experience (I have had Celiac Disease since 1986), my work history, and my educational background. I am, effectively, a trifecta. But that is really difficult to market well, since nobody knows where to put me. Everybody wants to recommend a specialist to their friends and family who come to them with a particular issue, so they don't think about me because I am all over the place. But what they are failing to realize is that, because I am all over the place, I'm very good at connecting dots. A good analogy for this is that a specialist is like a one-way street, and I am a five-way intersection.

There is nothing wrong with specialists, of course, because they know more than I do about their one particular specialty. But they have a hard time bridging gaps into any other form of health and wellness because that is not what they're trained in, so they aren't seeing the big picture regarding how one little thing somewhere else in the body can be directly affecting their specialty. This is where I come in. But getting people to grasp this has been difficult, to say the least.

I did hire a professional marketer in the spring of 2018 who helped me rebrand myself. She now has me specializing in Endocrine Disorders such as: Adrenal Fatigue, Hashimoto's, PCOS, Diabetes, Graves Disease, Hypoglycemia, and Hyperglycemia. While I am good at that, and the rebranding has helped bring in new clients under my better three-month package plan, this is still not me as a whole. I am so much more than this and can help with so many more health issues than this, so it makes me feel stifled. I get where she is coming from, and I tried it her way for a while. But, being such a diverse and adaptable creature makes it difficult for me to stay put in smaller boxes. It made more sense for me to run my business with more diversity and help as many people as possible. Therefore, I veered away from her paid advice and focus more now on creating delicious, quick, nutrient-dense, easy, budget friendly meals instead. I help people figure out how to do this with their more specific health issues and/or dietary restrictions in mind, while still sticking to a fairly regimented budget. This is an area of expertise I have cultivated throughout my many years of life experience and training. So, why wouldn't I pass this important information on to help others greatly improve their life, and sometimes finances, whenever I can?

On top of all of this, I designed my own website and maintain it so it doesn't get hacked. I have redesigned it a few times as I have grown. This includes adding in affiliates and then getting rid of most of them because I hadn't actually used their product. I decided I am very passionate about my authenticity and refuse to promote products I haven't used, even if they seem in line with my values and what I am writing.

I wrote a weekly blog for almost the first two years of the Adaptive Nourishment website and now have around 100 articles. Everything I write on my blog has to do with food, family, or finance, or some combination thereof. Although, since the rebranding, I have been focusing on creating more food content that's related to specific ailments instead of the other two topics. But I no longer write regularly, as the point was to get some cornerstone content on the website so people can use them as resources.

Oddly enough, though, my most popular article, by a landslide, is one I randomly wrote about kale bone. I was told about it during a trip to Atlanta and had to find out what the heck it was because it didn't make any sense to me. My article ranks higher than the restaurant that created it, which is how popular it is. If you're interested in checking out what the heck a kale bone is, here is the link to the article:

https://www.adaptivenourishment.com/world-kale-bone/

On top of all of this, Bryan and I embarked upon two more endeavors within my Adaptive Nourishment business. We started making a few custom food products for local farmers' markets and beer/wine stores to carry. These items included:

- Custom spice blends
- Custom popcorn blends
- Custom trail mix blends

We also did some custom essential oil blends for some of my clients and for a local herb shop, which was pretty cool. But we found that, with all of these, the profit margin was basically zero, and it was taking up too much of our time, so we put the kibosh on it after about a year. Everything we made in this genre, we put under our On Point subsidiary so that it was more of Bryan's baby than mine.

The second odd adventure was for us to be the caterers for a friend's wedding at a venue I had worked a few times for Irregardless and Rocky Top. I told her we didn't really do large-scale catering, but since I had run enough weddings, and Bryan had done commercial cooking, we were comfortable with it. The wedding was to be a little over 100 people, and the venue had a full kitchen, which is one of the reasons why I sent her there. Since we don't have a commercial kitchen, we couldn't legally make any of the stuff offsite, so if she wanted us to cater it, it would have to be at a venue with a kitchen. Overall, the wedding was beautiful, and the people we brought on to assist us, Bryan's old chef buddy, Xavier, and my old catering friend, Diane, worked out really well. I did reach out to one of my friends in the catering realm, to see if she had any bartenders she could spare who would be willing to work for cash, so I got a great guy from her. He was fantastic and didn't ask me for a thing the whole time. I would use him again in a heartbeat! I can tell you we didn't make much on the wedding at all because they negotiated us down to the bare minimum we could do. In all reality, I think the bartender made more than we did. But we were doing it more as a favor than anything else, so we were okay with that. However, weddings are a big undertaking, and it's not either of our preferences, so we don't advertise to anyone that we will cater a wedding. If somebody reaches out to us about it, then we may consider it, if the price is right, but other than that, no thank you!

Overall, my main business is still a work in progress. I haven't figured out the secret sauce yet, but I won't give up. My goal in life is to help as many people as I can to live their best lives to their highest potential. In order to do that, they have to feel and be well, and that is where I come in. After all, my tag line is "Creating healthier lives through dietary adaptation," and I stand by it!

### 49 — What I Learned

★ Creating a food video is much more difficult than I imagined

★ Designing a website can be a royal PITA (Pain in the Ass)

★ Maintaining a website and getting the right plugins can be a challenge

★ Figuring out the proper content for my audience has been difficult, due to my diversity

★ Affiliate links are not really my favorite thing, and so far, I haven't made any money off of them

★ Marketing effectively is a very difficult task, especially when you are as diverse as I am

★ Just because I have the trifecta of life experience, work experience, and education, it doesn't mean people will understand what I do and how I do it

★ Rebranding my health packages was extremely helpful because, before, I was severely undercharging for my services

★ Keep growing and learning because eventually I will hit upon the magic sauce

★ Rome wasn't built in a day, so persistence is key

# Irregardless Catering Sales

As I was graduating from my master's program, I was approached by one of the two owners of Irregardless about a potential full-time position in Catering Sales. They had seen my work ethic, attention to detail, customer relations, and skill over the past few years working for them and thought it would be a good fit. This was especially because I was finishing my master's and the other owner was looking for an in-house Nutrition Advisor to assist with menu items and choices for dietary restrictions. Plus, he was asked to speak regularly at different food conferences and thought I would be a good addition to his speaking engagements.

At first, I had to think about it because it would mean less freedom for me to come and go as I please. I realize this sounds like I am flaky, but that is not really the case. I worked myself to death on a regular basis, but it was on my terms, and if there was a week I needed to take off or didn't want to work as much because I had the kids, then, as I said before, I could. But they told me they would help me get my nutrition business off the ground by sending clients to me, which never happened, not even once.

I did end up agreeing, but under some conditions. The first condition was that I was still going to work for my mom once a week, so they could only have me four days a week. Everybody in the catering industry knows that you end up working most weekends, so they would really still have me five to six days a week. We ended up having a small negotiation because he originally offered me $38,000 and I wanted at least $40,000. We agreed to meet in the middle at $39,000, which breaks down to approximately $18.75 per hour and is more than what I had been making. However, it didn't really work out that way.

Even though we agreed I wasn't working for them on Thursday's, because I was working with my mom, they would call me and email me all day long with one emergency after another. And on top of it, I worked almost every weekend on Saturday and Sunday. Sometimes, I would have a Sunday off, but not that often. But wait, it gets better! We would have events at night that I booked, and they began requiring that the catering sales manager who sold it be there at the event for the entire time, which meant that, if I had my kids, I would have to bring them to the venue, and they would have to hang out the whole time, even on a school night. So I was really working closer to sixty hours a week for them instead of the forty that most salaries are predicated on. Therefore, my hourly rate broke down closer to $12.50 per hour, with *no benefits!* We didn't have vacation or sick time, nor did they have health insurance or a 401(k). Nothing. Nada. Zippo! This wasn't really a salary position in my experience, based on that information, but they didn't seem to grasp that.

I was also brought on to help with the documentation and creating policies and procedures because they had none in place when I came aboard. They were actively trying to grow the catering division of the company but had no processes, so they knew that, in order to do so, they would need some policies and procedures in place. Since I had a background in policies and procedures, they figured they had won the lottery. They were also using my interior design skills I had learned from growing up with my mother to help them redesign parts of the venue, as well as using my resources to create a custom rolling bar. I helped them do this based on the configuration of the rolling bars we used at The Umstead and the materials knowledge I had from working with my mom, as well as some of her resources. Of course, they weren't paying me any more money to work on this, nor were they paying me any more to go through every single menu item and designate the allergens. They just figured that, since I could do it, they shouldn't have to pay me extra for those services, even though nobody else could do it. This is a prime example of people continuing to try to take advantage of me for my diverse skill set but not wanting to compensate me properly for it.

So, when I came on, we had no contracts or document trails for anything. I began to create those, and we implemented contracts for all of us full-time employees that William, the GM, kept in his office. Before we created the contracts, though, we all had to sit down and discuss the bonuses for those three of us who were catering sales managers. According to Andrew, the owner, we were supposed to get a commission from every job we sold. Although he hadn't worked it out previously, we all decided that a payout every quarter would work, and it would be based on the quarterly sales of the prior quarter. He gave us each a sales goal and then a group goal, and if we met it, we would get our full commission, but if we didn't, we wouldn't get it. After the first quarter of this, the three of us sales managers decided this wasn't a really good plan because we all worked together as a cohesive team, including working each other's events, so one sales goal for us as a team was a better course of action than trying to pit us against each other. He agreed and implemented the plan, but never had us sign another contract. I talked to him about that aspect a few times, and he kept saying he would get around to it but not to worry about it because his word was good. Yeah, I never believe anybody's word if there isn't a paper trail to back it up. And this one did come back to bite me in the ass, just like I thought it would.

Besides not really ever having a day off, I didn't have any time to work on growing my business. You know, the one I went to grad school for and paid for out of my own pocket. Yeah, that one! On top of that, they weren't thrilled that I had a vacation planned to Peru for ten days and were giving me grief about it. But that trip had been planned and paid for at least six months prior to my working for them full-time, so that wasn't really my problem. I disclosed that information to them upon the initial conversations during our negotiation. They just forgot or were hoping I would change my mind. I can tell you that wasn't going to happen because I had been wanting to go to Machu Picchu for years now and wasn't about to let anybody stop me. Especially after I had already paid for it!

I had a ton of work to do before I left and tried to make sure all of my notes for any events I had during my trip were worked through to a tee so there weren't any issues while I was gone. When I got back, I had a ton of catch-up work to do, also. They said they weren't going to pay me for the time I was gone, but they ended up paying me partially for it, as a good-faith gift. Although, if you read back through any of the previous parts where I mention I was working every day and had no time off, then it wasn't really a good-faith gift. I was working overtime for them and not getting compensated for it, regularly. At least, that is my perspective on the situation, as well as both other catering sales managers at the time, Angela and Susan.

The kicker came when I was told that, if I took any more time off, I would have to schedule it on the wall calendar and run it by Angela, who was the catering sales director, first to get approval. I really hated this new rule because the three of us were pretty good at communicating with each other if we needed to be out so the others could pick up our slack. So, I planned a Sunday through Tuesday trip to Asheville with my new beau (now my permanent partner in crime), Bryan, a couple of months in advance. Angela approved it because I didn't have any events during that time. I scheduled it like that on purpose because we always had events on Saturdays, but Sunday through Tuesday were our slower times for events, so they wouldn't have to pick up any slack for me.

When the time came for our trip, I reminded the GM that I was going to be gone for those three days but that I would have the catering phone with me (as I was tethered to that stupid thing, also, day and night) Sunday through Tuesday, so I would still be answering calls from clients but just wouldn't be in the office. He asked me if I had told Andrew and Alicia, and I told him that I told them months prior when I booked the trip a Sunday through Tuesday but didn't remind them again recently because it was on the calendar.

When I left on that Sunday, I ended up on the phone with clients almost the whole drive there, and then I was on the computer working on an event for over an hour after we checked in. The next morning, I worked for a couple of hours and then had the phone with me all day, which seemed to ring incessantly. Bryan and I didn't actually get to spend much quality time together because I was working most of the freaking time!

As if this wasn't bad enough, it got worse. I got an email from Alicia that Tuesday morning, asking me who gave me permission to work remotely and that we would discuss it when I got back because it was unacceptable. Apparently, she had a hard time reading the calendar on which I marked off the days I would be gone on vacation. But in their minds, I didn't deserve vacation because they didn't give it. Well, I have news for you—everybody deserves a break from work. And for an industry that will kill you quickly if you let it, a break is needed every now and then because you end up working seven days a week. That is no quality of life!

I responded to her email and told her I went through the proper protocols to request the time off, and I put it on the calendar. She responded that she asked Angela and was told Angela didn't remember approving it. Now, I know this is a crock of shit, but Angela and Alicia had been having a personality conflict for quite some time because Alicia wanted to control Angela's life, also. Angela had a husband, also in the industry, and three kids, so she wasn't a fan of working seven days a week, either, and had it up to here with her bullying. So I know she was throwing me under the bus to save her job, even though only temporarily. And while I know that, it still kind of stung that she would do that to me, especially because we had worked together since my first days at Irregardless five years prior. But it is what it is. I saw the handwriting on the wall and knew I had to get out.

As soon as I got back in the office on Wednesday, I got back to work and doing my job, even though I was working the whole time I was gone. Everything ran as normal until Friday when I was called into a meeting by William and Angela. William told me they were going to revise the contracts for all catering sales managers. The new deal would be that we had to be in the office every day of the week, no matter what, and work our events whether they be nights or weekends. I told them that wasn't my deal when I got brought on, and I never would have come on board if that was what they were going to offer me. That was not the contract I signed, and I would not be working that schedule, period. William told me that, if I wanted to keep my job, I would have to sign it. I told him that wasn't going to happen, and if this was how they wanted to play it, then I would leave, and they could find another catering sales manager because I wasn't interested. He told me to think about it over the weekend and get back to him about it the following week. I told him I didn't have to think about it because I wasn't going to sign it. He told me, again, to think about it because they didn't want to lose me. Finally, I relented and told him I'd see him on Monday.

Monday went like every other day, but I was actively looking for a replacement for the income because I was going to put in my two-weeks' notice. However, I had booked a big event a couple of weeks out and didn't want to leave the other two ladies stranded. This was especially due to the fact that it was a fundraiser I had personal contacts with and got them to donate food because of our past relationship. This on top of the fact that my contact from Meals on Wheels and I were supposed to be giving a speech at the event together, so I didn't want to leave before that because the other two couldn't give the speech with him.

That Tuesday, I had about six different events and client meetings scheduled, so it was going to be a really *long* day. After my first two meetings, I found Andrew sitting in my office. He said we needed to talk, and I agreed that we did. He said our working relationship wasn't working well anymore and what did I have to say about that. I told him it wasn't working out because what I was doing and how much I was working was not the contract I signed and that it simply didn't work for me. He then told me it was time to part ways, and I agreed with him wholeheartedly. This position had been sucking the life out of me, and I didn't want anything to do with it anymore. He told me I didn't even have to work the rest of the day, to go ahead and pack up my stuff and leave. He does not like his pride to be hurt, in case you can't tell, and he is used to controlling people. So my telling him I wasn't going to do what he wanted, even though he changed the game, just really pissed him off and set off his control drama, since he is used to being an intimidator and getting his way. I was thrilled I didn't have to work myself to death for them anymore, but I felt bad for Angela and Susan because that left a lot of events of mine on their plate.

Ultimately, it didn't fully end there because he never paid me my commission for the sales I was a part of. I asked him and William both for my commission and was told by Andrew I didn't deserve them and that I didn't meet the sales quota. I reminded him that Angela, Susan, and I worked as a team and that we far more than exceeded the sales goal by almost double. I knew he had given Angela and Susan their sales commission because I talked to them about it, so it was only me that he refused to pay. So, I took him to the labor board because I get sick and tired of people taking advantage of me. Not only that but the two catering sales managers who were there prior to myself had been screwed out of commission by him, also, so this wasn't the first time he had done it. In all reality, my commission was only about $2,000, so it wouldn't have killed him to pay it. It took the labor board a couple of months to get back to me about the claim. When they did get back to me, they told me he produced some documents saying that commission was waived if the company didn't make any money. I asked them for proof that I signed it, and they said he didn't provide any signed copies, to which I told them he couldn't because that document didn't exist while I was there. Unfortunately, they sided with the business side, even though I produced my signed contracts because he *made documents up!* I was pissed, to say the least. Because, if you recall, part of what they brought me on to do was to create policies and procedures, of which they had none before I joined them. At least, I gave him a run for his money and made his life uncomfortable for a little while, even if I didn't get the commission I worked my ass off for. My only hope is that the experience taught him to create well documented policies and procedures and get everything signed. But I really can't tell you because, shortly after my departure, Angela and Alicia had their final showdown, and Angela left. She had been there at least seven years but couldn't put up with it anymore, and I don't blame her one bit.

I don't regret the experience, but it is certainly not one I want to experience again.

**50**

**What I Learned**

| | |
|---|---|
| ★ | Get everything in writing |
| ★ | Stop letting people take advantage of me for all of my diverse skill sets and refuse to compensate me appropriately for them |
| ★ | Some people just lack integrity, no matter how you slice it |
| ★ | Work-life balance is so much more important than a job |
| ★ | Stop putting my life's calling on hold to work for other people's dreams, for chump change at that |
| ★ | I will not be bullied |

# iMark Interactive

Right about the time I knew I needed to leave Irregardless, my brother was at the point with his business, iMark Interactive, where he needed to bring on some help. He offered me $30 an hour to help him with a few different aspects of the company, but he only needed me for a few hours a week.

The first thing he wanted me to help him with was rebranding his monthly subscription packages. He was changing the rates—although they are still ridiculously low for the level of service he provides—but he needed some new catchier names for each package. We spitballed in his office for a couple of hours about all of it, and it came to me! His company is called iMark, which reminds me of a marksman. What does a marksman do? They shoot bows and arrows. Well, he just happened to have four packages, so it made sense to me that the largest package be called "Bullseye," but I wasn't sure yet what to call the other three packages. So, we tossed that around, and then it made complete sense that the other three packages, from lowest to highest, would be "Ready," "Aim," and "Fire." He loved it and thought they worked well, so those are the names his four packages still have today.

The company he created, through many years of blood, sweat,

tears, and really long nights is a WordPress Maintenance and Support company. He not only has a website and a free course about how to use WordPress but he supplies services to those of us using the platform for our websites.

WordPress is a much easier platform to create a website on than the previous servers that only use HTML format. I love it because it makes creating a website and the content so much easier than before WordPress existed. There are definitely some nuances to WordPress, just like everything else. Now, instead of hard coding things in, you can upload a plugin to perform that specific task for you. This makes life so much simpler, as there is a plugin for just about every function you could desire, sort of like an app for your phone.

But these plugins are created by different developers, and as time goes on, they update the plugins for different functionality or to fix bugs. When this happens, you have to manually update each plugin to ensure it's the most recent version for full functionality on your website. But sometimes, the plugin updates can wreak havoc with other plugins or your theme and can crash your site. This is where a company like my brother's comes into play because, for all of our monthly subscribers, we maintain their plugins and ensure they are all working properly on their site with every other plugin. If we run across an issue, then we fix it if we are able to, or roll the plugin back to the previous version until the developer fixes the new bug with a new release. This is similar with WordPress updates, as they update the server regularly. Sometimes, the update WP releases can cause issues with certain plugins, so we have to watch for that carefully, also.

The other thing we do is run regular full-site backups, in case the site owner or we end up crashing their site and can't recover it through the c-panel or FTP. We also run extra security to keep hackers out of the sites we manage, and as a bonus, Grayson, my brother, is a WP guru and can fix pretty much any problem thrown his way. He is self-taught and has been working on the WP platform since it came out, so he understands it better than anybody else I know.

Our clients can submit tickets through our ticketing portal for any issues they're having, which can range between changing the font size and color of one area of text to installing a whole new theme and setting it up properly. And, of course, everything in between.

Grayson has taught me a lot, but there is still a ton I don't know, and to be honest, he is the guru, and it's his superpower, not mine. I do run the weekly plugin updates and double-check the backups for him. I also do some small one-off jobs when they come in, if they are up my alley, but most of it falls to him because he's much more tech savvy in this realm than I am.

The other thing he brought me on to do was to write two articles a month on one of his other websites, Debt Roundup. On this website, I wrote about anything financial that had to do with debt or getting out of debt. This was pretty easy for me, and I loved it! After I had written for him for about a year and a half, he asked me to stop so I could spend more time helping him with the tech stuff for iMark Interactive instead.

My brother and I work very well together, and I can do it wherever I have a secure connection, so I don't argue. I do my best to help him out with whatever is in my wheelhouse, and when my schedule allows, but sometimes I definitely feel like I'm letting him down because I am simply not as well versed in this area as he is. I still work with him today and plan to continue to do so until a time when he doesn't want or need me anymore. After all, we are family, and family is supposed to help each other out.

**51**

**What I Learned**

★   WP has a lot more idiosyncrasies than most people realize

★   The WP platform is so much easier than HTML

★   More about how SEO works today

★   How to fix a buggy file in c-panel

★   How to implement redirects

★   How to perform an SSL migration, most of the time

★   My brother is much smarter than me in this realm

# Brickstone Properties & Management

Less than a month after Irregardless and I parted ways, I was recommended by a friend to this property management company. They were a small business she worked for full-time, getting their books in order for their multiple entities, but they needed some big-time help with a few other things on a part-time basis. Basically, they had been offloading everything on her, and she finally got them to see there was no way one person could handle all of the tasks they kept trying to throw on her plate. So, one of the owners, Tom, agreed to bring somebody else in. She pushed for me to be brought on, since she and I have worked together in the past and she knew my work ethic and skill set. Tom finally reached out to me, and we agreed to meet up for coffee the morning of my birthday to have an in-person meeting and see if I was a good fit.

We met up at Starbucks for about an hour, and he explained they had multiple entities in multiple states and owned/managed approximately 600 properties in six different states. That was a pretty decent sized portfolio! They needed somebody to help Erin, my friend, with the books, as well as to handle all utilities, and he thought it would be approximately fifteen hours a week. That sounded like cake to me!

We discussed money, and I told him I wanted $20 an hour. but he was more comfortable with $16. We agreed to meet closer to the middle at $17.50 to start with and see how it went, and then we could revisit it. I agreed to start the next Monday and to come into their makeshift office that was just down the road from my house, to train with Erin on the processes for a few days. But after that, my schedule was up to me, as long as I got the work done. I wasn't required to come into an office because none of them did regularly. SOLD!

So, now, I had three jobs in less than a month after leaving Irregardless, I was making more money, working less, and didn't have to go into an office, other than my mother's, on a regular basis. This is what I call a win-win! I literally had one day off in between parting with Irregardless and getting the work with my brother and increasing my work with my mom to two days a week. That is how crazy this is!

But back to the Brickstone part of the story. I went into the office and trained with Erin the first few days, and then I was good to go. She set me up with the remote server that hosts the different sets of Quickbooks that we use for different entities, as well as loaded AppFolio (this is the property management software platform we use) onto my computers. She gave me a quick tour of it but told me Courtney, the regional manager, could give me a better tour of the platform if I wanted to sit with her for a little bit. Of course, I did, so she gave me a more in-depth lesson, which has been extremely useful in the subsequent years I have worked for this company. Erin then showed me where the mailbox key was and walked me out to the mailbox so we could check the mail. She said that was something we needed to do regularly while the other owner, Jerry, was out of the country. But once he was back, he controlled the mail and had it sent to his house because he liked to keep tabs on it. I hate to say this but that is really freaking weird and controlling behavior, and to top it off, it makes everybody's life difficult. Once he got back into the country and found out they had brought me on, he wanted to meet me in person, and during that meeting, he informed me I would have to come pick up the mail from his house once a week. They would pay me the whole time I had to do that and pay my mileage, but it has been a continual PITA. There are just so many easier ways to get mail delivered that it doesn't make any sense, other than the fact that he feels a deep-seated need to go through every single piece of mail before he hands it over. I just really don't understand this one. But that's how it goes, and I move on.

Besides inputting all of the utilities into the system (and we are talking electric, water, and gas), I had to learn the interesting idiosyncrasies of each utility company in each municipality. Enter in Excel spreadsheets! Have I mentioned that I love spreadsheets? Erin does, too, which is one of the nerdy things we have in common. I created a spreadsheet that listed:

- Each utility company
- Their contact info
- Whether or not they have a website (yes, not all of them do!)
- Our login info, if we are able to log in
- Whether or not a deposit is required
- The amount of the deposit
- If we can pay online without a fee
- What special instructions are necessary for the setup of that specific utility

While this may sound like a lot of steps, this information is all very important to get things done! Plus, when I get to the point where I leave the company, this should be a very good tool for whoever takes over my position. And at one point, I did leave, and it did help the person temporarily taking over, which was Courtney. Poor Courtney! But that comes a little bit later in the story.

On the same spreadsheet, under different tabs, I had the utility status for each property, as well as the date it was turned on or off, for billing purposes. You see, if a tenant moves in and doesn't switch the utilities into their name, I have to turn off the utilities, which I don't like to do. But at the same time, our contracts say they are responsible for all utilities. I don't always catch the utility usage still being in our name until I get a bill because lack of communication is a rampant continuing issue at this company, and people forget to tell me when they move people in. I tried to implement a few different strategies to get the PM's (Property Managers) to let me know when they moved a tenant in, but until they grant me the use of a cattle prod, they won't work. So most of the time, I caught the usage when I saw the next bill, double-checked the move-in date of the tenant, turned off the utilities, and informed the PM that I have them scheduled to be turned off, so they need to let their tenant know to shake their butt and apply for service if they want things like electricity, water, and gas. Then, once the final bill showed up, I would post it to the tenant page in AppFolio, as well as a note stating how much they owed us for services used, and Courtney would post it to their ledger. Let the good times roll!

I was also in charge of trash services if we ever needed them, which was rare, and that is yet another tricky animal. Some companies required that we physically go into the office and hand them a check. Well, that's a bit difficult to do when you are states away, in the corporate office. I really don't understand why some of these utility companies are so antiquated in their processes, when others, who do the same bloody thing, can figure it out just fine. Seriously, people, what is the problem here?

Not too long after I started, though, they began to throw other tasks at me. They realized I have a background in policies and procedures (yep, here we go again!), and since they didn't have any, they would love my help creating them. They were paying me hourly, so all that meant was more hours, so they were technically paying me to work on these, but it was still annoying that they began to put more tasks on me once they realized I could do it, but they were unwilling to bump up my pay. Same story as other jobs in the past.

Courtney, Erin, and I collaborated about the policies and procedures quite a few times in a four-to-five-month period. Once we got a document completed that we were all satisfied with, we would call a meeting with Tom and Jerry to get their approval for the release. That always turned into a nightmare because the two of them can't agree and have completely different perspectives on things. I had to explain to them what a Rev (revision) was and how, once documents get released, you leave it out there in circulation for preferably a year and then release a new Rev with changes. It is very difficult to get anybody to follow any sort of new policy or procedure if you put it out there, train them on it, tell them it will be reinforced, and then two weeks later, release a new Rev with conflicting information. I call this bad parenting! Because running a company is similar to parenting, in that you have to run the show, make all of the rules, and make sure the children are doing what you told them to do. Children, just like employees, look up to their parents for advice and guidance. They also model behavior. So, if you don't run the company well (aka parenting), then you have unruly children, and the company will ultimately fail.

I told them this, and explained it to them logically, but they just weren't getting it. After this happened a few times, they told us to stop working on policies and procedures for now and that they would let us know when we could revisit it again. It has been over a year and a half, and we still have no active policies or procedures. The motto for everyone around this company, except for the two owners, is "Not my monkey, not my zoo." I am hoping it's starting to become clear as to why that is the motto, at this point.

The other things they started to have me work on were nuisance violations and nuisance liens resulting from violations. Anytime a violation came in, I would create a WO (Work Order) in AppFolio on the property page, or sometimes the tenant page, depending upon whether or not the property was occupied or vacant, and then email it out to the PM for that property with a list of infractions, the date of the violation, and when it was supposed to be cured. The PM would then communicate with me to let me know the action plan, when it was expected to be cured, and then when it was cured so I could reach out to the officer in charge to get it re-inspected. Once it was cleared from the officer, I would note it in my spreadsheet as cured and close out the WO in AppFolio. This might sound like it shouldn't be that difficult, but it was like herding cats! If we ended up getting a lien because we didn't get the violation until after the cure date (please see the section about the mail being hostage), then I would have to confirm that "the boys" wanted me to pay it and execute payment.

It's at this point, I should mention that, when I first came aboard, I introduced them to this lovely e-check system called Deluxe E-checks. They are FDIC insured and have an extension for Quickbooks so you can execute the checks through QB, and it will email your vendors directly. The vendor can then print out the check on any type of paper they want, take it to the bank, and cash it. Some banks will even recognize the check with their deposit function on their apps, but I have noticed that is only the larger banks, whereas the smaller banks don't seem to have that capability yet. This is a system I found for my mother's business when we were looking for another check option because they are so darn expensive, and we rarely use them. These checks, at this point in time, cost $.10 per check, and you purchase them in sets of 100 and up. They aren't physical checks, though, so they have an online portal that will show you all of the checks you have written, how many checks you have left, let you reprint or resend a check to somebody, or void a check. It's a beautiful system, and I love it at all of the businesses I have gotten this technology for. But government agencies are a little slow on the uptake, and I've noticed that most of them have no clue what an e-check is, even though this technology has been around for years, so they won't take them. Some of my utility companies are in the same antiquated boat, which makes things even more difficult if they don't have an online payment portal. With regard to nuisance liens, if they don't have an online payment portal so I can pay with a debit card, I have to track down Tom and tell him to write a physical check (because he has a physical checkbook hidden somewhere for emergencies), and then I have to go meet him somewhere to get it. It's a ridiculous process for something that could be so simple if these older agencies would just wake up and smell the e-checks!

On top of all of these tasks, Courtney trained me how to adjust a tenant's ledger in AppFolio for their rental rate. I would get letters from different Section 8 agencies when a renewal had been completed or a rent adjustment, for some other reason, and I needed to change how much a tenant owed us versus Section 8. This wasn't too hard to do once she showed me where it was located in AppFolio. So, whenever I got those notices in, I would scan and save the notice, upload it to the documents section of the tenant page, adjust the ledger with the correct date for the change to occur, and put a note in stating what I had done and when the effective date of change was. Then I would send an email to Courtney and the PM for that property, informing them there was a rent adjustment for that tenant.

I also started helping Erin with entering the vendor invoices from one of our emails on a weekly basis. I had to go through the inbox of that particular email and enter all of the invoices. But it was a little bit more time consuming than that because, for each invoice that came in, I had to go into AppFolio and find the matching WO for it so it could be noted in QB on the memo line. Then, I had to upload the invoice into the WO and close it out, if it was ready to be closed out.

Entering rent rolls was another fun addition to my plate. We had a few third-party property managers for certain cities, so they would send me our monthly statements. I then had to put them in the correct set of books with the correct properties listed under the "class" section so everything was properly recorded. With the properties we were managing, I had to go into our bank accounts and upload the most recent statement and then compare it to the rent rolls recorded in AppFolio, to find out which property went with which payment. Those had to be recorded in two different sets of books. Is this sounding extremely fun and exciting to you yet?

The next fun task was to learn about property taxes and how to request an appeal. With a little over 600 properties in six states, this was a full-time job for somebody else. The boys wanted me to look at every property that came in and see if the municipality was increasing the property taxes. If so, they wanted me to appeal the decision so we could potentially get reduced taxes on each property. This definitely required a massive spreadsheet, and I created it with tabs for each different county in each state. This thing is a beast! This is how I have each tab laid out:

- Parcel ID or RE#
- Property Address
- Property Configuration & Sq. Ft.
- Market Value the previous year
- Assessed Value the previous year (the taxes are based on the assessed value)
- Proposed Market Value
- Proposed Assessed Value
- Percentage Increase this year from last year
- Comps
- Notes (such as house fire, no electrical, flooded, HVAC missing, etc.)

This information would be inputted as I got the tax assessments in, which started around August of each year. Once I had enough information for each county and had decided which ones to appeal, I would begin submitting my appeals. Each county had a website where the appeals needed to be submitted, but I found out through the process that, the more information such as pictures showing damage, the better my chances were of getting an appeal granted. Some counties had the inspector in charge call me directly, discuss the property, and adjust it over the phone. If they all could only be that simple! Most of them weren't like that, though. I found that becoming friends with the Property Tax Assessor in Jacksonville, Florida was extremely helpful because we had about half of our properties in just that one area. But the property tax assessors in Atlanta and surrounding areas were completely different—not only from Jacksonville but from each other, also. I say that Atlanta is a free-for-all because I found out they don't have any state law capping how much a municipality can increase property taxes in one year, so it's like the Wild West down there. At least in Jax, it was capped at 6% each year, so I knew if it went beyond that, then I had a case. Either way, there were a lot of idiosyncrasies to learn here, and I became pretty good at figuring out which properties to file appeals for and which ones to leave alone, as well as the unique processes for each location. But this was extremely time-consuming for the last half of the year.

And to top it off, they then began having me file insurance claims for storm damage to our properties in Florida, from Hurricane Irma. This was an interesting process to learn because we had so many damaged that it made sense for us to find somebody to advocate for us. I found out the insurance they were carrying on most of our properties was underinsured, so that caused a recurring issue. We decided I should look into finding a public adjuster to help us facilitate this. A public adjuster is somebody who is the advocate for you in the situation of an insurance claim against the insurance company. They are almost like lawyers, but not really. They know the ins and outs of the rules and laws of property insurance, so they are great people to have on your side if an insurance company is screwing you around, which they are notorious for. I did some digging—because that is one of my favorite things to do—and found a few adjusters that could handle claims in the Jax area. After speaking with them and getting the information regarding how they operated, I sent a list of the two I liked to Jerry and Tom. To be honest, my first choice was this man named Liam, so he was who I was hoping they would go with. After a few days, they got back to me and told me they had decided to go with Liam, so Liam and I would be in contact, regarding any and all insurance claims and how to handle everything. That worked for me! Liam was fantastic and extremely knowledgeable. He was our saving grace on all of these claims because of how our insurance had been set up. The way he operated is that he didn't get paid until we got money back from the insurance company for a claim, and then he got a certain percentage. So, it was in his best interest to get us the largest amount possible because that got him more money. This was a pretty long process, as we had multiple claims, but it was successful, overall. We haven't had to use him for other claims, at this point, but we might have to in the future. But now, I know how things are done, courtesy of him, so it makes it easier for me to file one claim that's not as intricate. I appreciate him and his expertise for opening my eyes to the world of property insurance claims.

As you can tell, the amount of things they threw upon me well exceeded the original discussion of utilities management and some QB work. Most weeks, I was working more like thirty to forty hours a week for them, which I really didn't like because I had other work for other people to do. I asked for a raise at the ninety-day mark and got crickets, even though I asked twice. They pretended not to hear and/or remember me asking. So, on my birthday the following year, I called Tom directly and told him it had been a year since I was hired. I was hired for one thing and had taken on a whole host of other things, which was fine, but I needed to be compensated accordingly for successfully taking on more work. He asked what I wanted, and I told him $20 an hour, which was way too low. I should have asked for $25, but that was already a decent raise. More so than I ever got at any corporate job. This would have been fine for a little while, but I knew I was going to have to ask for more, based on all of the things they kept throwing at me.

It was around this time that Erin had enough of the lack of communication and sheer unorganization of the company and found herself a better paying, more organized company she could work for from home, so she told them she was quitting. She did give them notice, and they asked her if she could please stay on a few hours a week, just to do the payroll and reconciliation reports. She agreed to that, but they were going to have to hire people to replace her because she had been doing the job of two people, like all the rest of us. They started working on hiring people and didn't even talk to me or Courtney about the qualifications necessary, which ticked me off. The first two people they brought in were horrible. The woman was there for one day of training and then never showed back up. The man, Jorge, came in with a bravado that he knew everything and that he was going to fix everything that was wrong. I greatly detest people who come into a situation, not knowing anything about it, and directly assume they are smarter than those familiar with the situation. I don't like to be underestimated, and I certainly don't like it coming from a chauvinistic male. As you can tell, we didn't really hit it off, but he didn't hit it off with any of the females who worked for the company, either. The deal with him was that he kept disappearing to Jax and Atlanta and not actually showing up on job sites or doing anything other than hanging out at bars and going on dates with women he met on Tinder. He was freaking horrible, and we all kept trying to tell the boys he wasn't actually doing anything but milking them dry. They didn't want to believe they had made such an error in judgment, so they dug their heels in and stuck by him for a few months. Luckily, they came to their senses after about three months of this nonsense and fired him. Thank you!

The next three they hired stayed on for a little while longer, but we weren't fans of them, either. There was nothing wrong with their personalities, but their work ethic and brain cell function left a lot to be desired. One of them, Monica, was taking over the maintenance part that Erin had been handling. She had owned her own business, doing maintenance work before this, but had never worked in an office. While she had great skills in dealing with the tenants, she couldn't figure out her way around a computer to save her life. Which, unfortunately, was a necessity for this job because you had to enter WO's, update them, and close them out. She lasted maybe six months. Katie was the one they hired to help with admin stuff such as going through the mail, scanning it, and doing odd things for us. While she had a very sweet personality, she just couldn't figure out how to do basic things like scanning properly or reading documents. Problem-solving was not a skill she had. She was better suited for a corporate environment where her daily tasks were limited to a prescribed amount of fairly mundane things. This sort of environment was just not a good fit for her because she lacked problem-solving skills which are essential in any small business environment.

Amy was the third hire, and she was there the longest, much to my dismay. She was also very sweet but tried to compensate for her lack of common sense and problem-solving skills by being overly sweet.

That has never worked for me because I can see right through it. I am simply not a fan. I wanted nothing to do with her or Katie because all they did was create more work for me. Neither one of them could effectively read a spreadsheet or scan documents correctly, nor could they properly enter data in AppFolio. And don't get me started on the books! Katie claimed she had a degree in accounting; well, I beg to differ. She couldn't figure out her way around QB to save her life; she continually entered data in incorrectly. They were making me lose my damn mind, and I wasn't even in the office! Amy ended up staying on about seven months, which was seven months too long, in my opinion. All three of them would sit around the office and play on their phones and talk most of the day, which was not actually getting any work done. It was no wonder they were so inefficient!

This was all coming to a head with me because I had simply had enough. Right before I left for Jamaica with my family in January, I had a come-to-Jesus meeting with Tom. I told him I was done but that I would stay on to help train somebody if they wanted me to. He asked me why, and I told him I simply couldn't work with the three stooges because they made my life, and everybody else's life, so much more difficult. They were creating more work for us than they were help-ing to alleviate, and he was basically burning his money up by paying them to sit there and do nothing full-time. On top of that, I was highly offended that he was paying Amy more than me, when she was only using the processes I created, and she wasn't even doing it effectively, so Courtney and I had to continually go back behind her and fix her mistakes. If that was how little he thought of me, then he could have them for more money, and I was out. It was a much longer chat than that, but I basically "mommed" him, which he said he didn't like. I told him to stop acting like a child and I wouldn't have to, and he agreed.

Basically, I was gone for three weeks, and Courtney begged him multiple times to bring me back because she couldn't handle everything I did, nor did she know how to do it. Even with my notes and spreadsheets, everything I had been doing was intricate and difficult, and I did it very efficiently. Because I am good with numbers and can save them in my head, I didn't have to go back to find an EIN number, bank account number, cc number, or most property addresses because they were saved in my head. Hell, I even knew some of the numbers for the utility companies I called on a regular basis in my head! She had a major breakdown and told him she just couldn't do it and Thing 1 and Thing 2 (Katie and Amy) have proven they can't do it, either, and were just making her life more difficult. He finally called me and asked me how much I wanted in order for me to come back. I told him $30 an hour, to which he balked at. He said he would have to talk to Jerry but that he didn't think he would agree to that. I reminded him that, for the hours I work, that still equals less than he was paying Amy to sit on her butt in the office and do nothing. He came back to me a day later and said that was too high but that they really needed me back. I told him I was drawing the line at $27.50 because they wanted to only pay me $25, and that was my final offer. Take it or leave it. He said he would get back to me, and I told him it was his decision, but that was where I was standing. He got back to me a few hours later and agreed.

So this is where we are now, at $27.50 per hour. But my terms were that I wasn't working with Thing 1 and Thing 2 (who are no longer with us, thankfully) and that I would only be handling the utilities portion. He agreed to those terms, and I began working for them again. My real ulterior motives, besides beefing up our savings account, were to help

Courtney diversify herself with a broader skill set. It has worked, and now the company is down to the boys, Courtney and myself, and my favorite PM in Atlanta, Shannon. I don't know how much longer I will be with them because they still continually ask me to do stupid stuff and have a huge issue with lack of communication, but for now, I am still helping out.

**52**

**What I Learned**

★ How to deal with different utility companies and their sometimes-odd processes

★ The rules around filing property tax appeals

★ What constitutes as an actual property comp and what doesn't

★ How to file a property insurance claim

★ What public adjusters do and how awesome they are

★ How to use the AppFolio system

★ How to enter rent rolls

★ Not everybody understands what a Rev is or how often to release documents for maximum efficacy

★ How nuisance violations and nuisance liens work

★ I have to stop letting people know how much I am capable of doing and how efficient I am because they keep taking advantage of me

★ My diverse skills are worth much more than I give myself credit for

# Whisk

Bryan had done a few cooking classes at a local kitchen supply store called Whisk. They had a fantastic open concept,
teaching kitchen at the back of the store where they held
regular classes, as well as events. When he told me about
this, I thought it would be a great idea for us to host one together
and combine our skills. He reached out to the manager, and they
were excited by the idea because they didn't have any vegetarian or
gluten-free chefs on their staff. So they set up a time for us to come in
and speak with them about our idea for food choices.

We didn't meet with the owners but, instead, met with the woman who
was in charge of booking the classes, Martha. She liked our idea and told
us it would be great if we could do something for Valentine's Day because
that was one of their busiest times to book classes. We came up with a few
ideas, which she tweaked incessantly. She kept sending us back suggestions
and edits to our recipes, which was annoying because we were the chefs.
There were also a few dish ideas that she pooh-poohed, even though they
worked really well with the other choices we were presenting.

When the time finally came for us to teach the first class, it was a mad-
house of prep work once we arrived. They did provide two volunteers to

help us prep, serve, and clean up, but there really wasn't any training to speak of, with regard to how they like to do things. Bryan and I work really well together as a team, and we came up with some great stuff. Here are a few of the recipes that people kept raving about:

## VEGETARIAN MASSAMAN CURRY

**Ingredients:**

- 2 Cups Cauliflower (chopped)
- 1 Cup Coconut Milk
- ¾ Cup Water
- ½ Cup Carrots (Sliced)
- ½ Cup Onion (Sliced)
- ½ Cup Green Beans (Chopped)
- ½ Red Bell Pepper (Chopped)
- 3 Cloves Garlic (Minced)
- 3 Tbsp Peanut Butter
- 2 Tbsp Red Curry Paste (Preferably Thai Kitchen)
- 1 Tbsp Cane Sugar
- 2 tsp Coconut Oil
- 2 tsp Ginger (minced)
- ½ tsp Tamarind Concentrate
- ½ tsp Sea Salt
- ¼ tsp Cardamom
- ¼ tsp Cayenne
- ¼ tsp Cinnamon
- ¼ tsp Cumin
- ¼ tsp Star Anise
- 1/8 tsp Cloves

**Instructions:**

1. In large pan, add oil and heat to medium, then add onions

2. Cook for 4 minutes

3. Add bell pepper, cauliflower, garlic, ginger, green beans, and half of the salt

4. Mix, cover, and cook for 4 minutes

5. Add carrots, curry paste, and spices

6. Cook for 2 minutes

7. Add peanut butter, sugar, tamarind, coconut milk, water, and remaining salt

8. Mix well and cook for 6 - 8 minutes until the curry thickens and the veggies are tender

9. Serve over Ginger Coconut Jasmine Rice

**Yield: 4 servings**

# FORBIDDEN RICE

## Ingredients:

- 2 cups Coconut Water
- 1 cup Black Rice
- 1 Tbsp Coconut Oil
- 1 Tsp Sea Salt
- 1 Bay Leaf

## Instructions:

1. Rinse rice well and soak for 10 minutes
2. Rinse rice again
3. Bring coconut water to a boil
4. Add rice, oil, salt, and bay leaf
5. Reduce to simmer and cover for 20 - 30 minutes
6. Turn off heat and let sit for 5 minutes
7. Fluff and serve

**Yield: 4 servings**

# ORANGE AVOCADO SORBET

(This recipe requires a Vitamix, but a blender would work, also)

**Ingredients:**

- 5 Cups Ice Cubes
- 2 Oranges (Peeled and Halved)
- ½ Avocado
- ½ Lemon (Peeled and Seeded)
- ¼ Cup Agave Nectar or Honey
- 1 tsp Vanilla Extract
- Orange Peel
- Pistachios (crushed with a mallet or in a food processor)

**Instructions:**

1. Place all ingredients (except the ice cubes) into the Vitamix in the order listed
2. Select Variable 1
3. Turn machine on, quickly increase Variable 10, and then to High
4. Blend for 30 second on High
5. Add ice cubes and start back at Variable 1
6. Quickly increase to Variable 10 and then to High, as before
7. Use tamper to press ingredients into blades
8. The machine will begin to sound different in about 30 - 60 seconds and will form 4 mounds
9. Stop machine and serve
10. If desired, top with crushed pistachios

**Yield: 4 servings**

# AZTECA CHOCOLATE TRUFFLES

## Ingredients:

- 2/3 cup Heavy Cream
- 12 oz Chocolate (68% or higher)
- 1/3 cup Cocoa Powder
- 2 Tbsp Unsalted Butter
- Zest of 1 Orange
- 2 Cinnamon Sticks
- ½ Tsp Crushed Red Pepper
- 1/8 Tsp Cayenne Pepper
- 1/8 Tsp Sea Salt

## Instructions:

1. Bring cream, chocolate, orange, cinnamon, and peppers to a simmer
2. Let cool
3. Bring back to a simmer
4. Strain through fine mesh
5. Fold butter and salt
6. Let cool
7. Scoop and roll in cocoa

**Yield: 20 servings**

After our first class, the owners asked us to come in and speak with them because they wanted to give us feedback, as to how we did. They said they liked our energy together and that people really liked the recipe ideas. But they didn't like how Bryan didn't really interact with the participants much but, instead, was focused more on cooking. I was out in the audience, talking more to the participants and answering individual questions. They didn't like that, either. Although, this is usually how we divide and conquer. So we said we were open to suggestions, if they wanted us to modify our technique. They said we should both stay up front the whole time and only send the volunteers out into the audience but that we should have a defined question-and-answer session towards the end. We agreed that we would try that, which we did for the next session, and it worked out really well. They also said we didn't serve enough alcohol with each dish (because this was another aspect of what we had to do—define a pairing choice from a wine shop they designated and ensure we had enough wine for all participants), so we needed to make sure we refill at least once if participants ask. They said that participants paid a good amount of money to come to each class and had certain expectations with regard to the quantity received. We did that for the next class, and we didn't have very many requests for refills, so I'm still not really sure what they were talking about there.

Overall, we were on-site prepping, teaching the class, and breaking down for a little over six hours. Part of the requirement is that you also do your own grocery shopping, but they will either reimburse you or you can put it on their credit if you shop at a few of their approved stores. So the grocery shopping, including drive time, took about an hour and a half on average. Then, on top of that, we had to submit our recipe ideas (to which they usually require at least four different dishes and a dessert) for each event. After that, we had continual back-and-forth with Martha, changing or editing our recipe ideas and then trying to tweak the recipes. That whole part took anywhere from five to ten hours. Since they only pay each one of us $200 a piece for each class, that breaks down to something along the lines of $11.43 - $16.00 per hour. I hate to say this, but it really wasn't worth it! So, after four classes, we didn't go back and do anymore, and we are just fine with it. Our backgrounds and culinary skills are simply worth more compensation than that.

**53**

**What I Learned**

★ How much work goes into one cooking class

★ That $200 isn't really a lot of compensation per cooking class

★ How well Bryan and I work together to come up with recipes and present them

★ That I love to teach and talk about food even more than I thought I did!

# Freelance Writing

Istarted freelance writing with my brother on one of his websites, Debt Roundup, in case you do not recall from the earlier section. I love writing and always have, so to get paid for it is a huge bonus for me. It made me start thinking that it would be fantastic if I could get more people to start paying me to write articles about the topics I am well versed in. So I went on the hunt!

Here are the myriad of topics I can speak intelligently on:

- Nutrition
- Personal Finance
- Family
- Parenting
- Animal Nutrition
- Real Estate
- Medical Technology
- Accounting
- Credit Cards
- Divorce
- Home Improvement
- Travel

- Traveling on the Cheap
- Exercise
- Cooking and Baking
- Vegetarian
- Gluten-Free
- The list goes on!

The first freelance writing gig I got was for a website called Living on the Cheap, which was about frugal living. This happens to be one of my go-to topics, so it was a good fit. She only agreed to pay me $50 an article, which I knew was low, but for my first real freelance writing gig, outside of my blog and writing for my brother, I figured what the hell. I only ended up writing two articles for her because she was flaky as hell. She wouldn't respond, was very slow to pay, wouldn't tell me when things were going to go live so I could share the articles on social media, etc. She requested I pitch an idea to her every time before writing, which I did, but then she wouldn't get back to me. I just got tired of dealing with her and stopped trying to hunt her down.

After I got back from FinCon, I got a few other gigs for financial writing. So, I wrote for Chime, Bigger Pockets (see the next section), a lawyer, and Frugal Farmer. The rates ranged anywhere from $40 an article to $350 an article. None of these ended up being long-term, though, with the exception of Frugal Farmer, which I am still writing for today. Sadly, that one happens to be one of the lower paying gigs.

I also got invited to be a part of the professional panel for an Inceptia webinar on food insecurity on college campuses. I was really excited about that one, but then I found out it wasn't paid, either. What is it with everybody and pro bono stuff? It's really difficult to make a living when everybody wants me to do everything for free. I did do the webinar and really enjoyed it, but I can tell you I haven't seen one single spike in traffic, nor have I gotten any new clients from it, so I feel like it was an ultimate bust.

At this point, I wouldn't mind getting one or two stable freelance writing gigs on the higher end of the $350 per article, just so I can get more content out there and continue to do what I love. But the biggest issue for me is that I am so diverse with my areas of expertise that people have a hard time placing me, so they just bypass me. Narrowing down my niches is something I have tried to do, but it doesn't seem to change the outcome much because people see my writing in many different places, in multiple genres. This is my ultimate challenge!

**54**

**What I Learned**

★ Freelance writing is one of my passions

★ Getting a freelance writing gig is not as easy as it sounds, even if you are a good writer and already have one book published

★ The pay rates for freelance writing are all over the place, so it's good to go into it with eyes wide open

★ Being so diverse with your areas of expertise can really bite you in the ass

# BellBert Investments, LLC

I have always been interested in real estate but have never been in a position to be able to purchase anything other than my primary residence. That is, until after I sold the property I had for fifteen years in the downtown area and made a pretty decent profit. With that profit, I was able to put down almost 50% on another larger house, with an in-ground pool for us and the kids, pay off my existing loans, and put some money away in savings. Once we got to that point, the idea of buying real estate came back in full force to the front of my mind. While I was at the FinCon conference in 2017, I started talking to some other real estate investors and was introduced to Bigger Pockets, the largest real estate investing website in the world. I got involved in a couple different round-table discussions and decided I was going to try to find a way to figure out how to get into buy-and-hold properties.

A lot of real estate investors make this sound like it's so much easier than it really is. So don't believe that bunch of hooey! If it was that simple, then everybody would be doing it. Common sense tells you this, so please believe it. We didn't have much capital to begin with, so I had to start trying to figure out financing options.

The first thing I tried was hard money lenders, which are a whole different animal than the lenders I had been used to; they are more willing to lend money out for real estate, but they are always higher interest loans than you would find with a conventional mortgage, and they are pretty darn short-term. This type of loan works well for people who are in the fix-and-flip business, but that wasn't us.

I looked tirelessly for conventional mortgages but no banks had a tolerance for it or wanted to play with us because we didn't have any properties yet. That was when I decided to talk to my banker at the small bank I use for my Adaptive Nourishment business, and she gave me another solution. It is a really great thing to have wonderful connections with your banker, and Shryl is no exception to this rule. She told me I could probably apply for a HELOC because we had enough positive equity in our house from putting down so much when we purchased it. So, I applied for a HELOC, and within two weeks, we were granted $52,000. Once we had that set in stone, I started hitting the ground hard for a property that fit my parameters in Fayetteville, North Carolina, which was my chosen market for a myriad of reasons. After searching for a couple of weeks, we finally found one that worked for us, got under contract, and closed by the end of the year. Yes, I am told that I moved like greased lightning and no grass grows under my feet. This is probably pretty darn accurate!

Bigger Pockets asked me to start writing on their site after we met at the FinCon conference, and I was excited to do so, especially because I was freelance writing, so I was under the impression this would be a paid gig. Not so much! They didn't tell me until after I got in that it was pro bono and to help increase my network in the real estate investors market because the more people that know you and trust you, the easier it is to get deals. I can't say I have found that to be true yet, but it could be because I don't put all of my eggs in one basket, so I don't have a ton of time to devote to networking. However, if you want to read more about my story and how we got started in real estate investing, then this is a great article to check out:

https://www.biggerpockets.com/renewsblog/finally-started-investing-real-estate/

This one is another great one I wrote for their site that tells you more about the first investing mistake we made that cost us money, and how we won't repeat the same mistake again:

https://www.biggerpockets.com/renewsblog/our-first-investing-lesson/

Basically, Bryan and I decided we would own this business together, since the plan is for it to be a big part of our retirement, as passive income. So we named the company BellBert, LLC as a combination of both of our last names. Mine is Bell and his is Joubert, so there you go! Although, it is pronounced Bell Bear, not Bert, because his last name is Creole French. I basically run this entity, but Bryan puts his two cents in when I ask him for it. I take care of the research, finding property management, dealing with maintenance issues, setting up utilities, paying property taxes, keeping the books, paying for insurance, etc. I am also the one who works on paying back the HELOC monthly from our tenant's rent that is deposited into our BellBert, LLC bank account from our property management company.

Right now, we only have one rental property, but our goal is to get at least ten in the next couple of years, or some multiplexes. This is so we can have the loans paid off by the time our youngest one leaves for college in about twelve years. This is a lofty goal, I know, but I am hoping to either get some seller financing or get some bank to play with me for a bulk package mortgage. I guess only time will tell!

★    Real estate investing is much harder than it looks

★    Finding the right market is key to any buy-and-hold success

★    Knowing what your limitations are before jumping into a deal is important

★    Knowing how many properties you want to attain for passive income is a magical number, and you should go into the game knowing this

★    Real estate investing is just a game, like the stock market, but with the potential for much more lucrative rewards if you do your due diligence

# Cash Wise Ex-Wives

Afriend of mine in the financial space, Kayla, and I had previously worked together on some projects and had an overlap of people we worked with. We also roomed together at FinCon (the awesome annual Financial Conference for all of us financial nerds) in 2017, so we got to know each other really well. During that conference, we learned a lot about each other and our personal lives. The fact that we were both divorced and female entrepreneurs was a strong bond for us. We kept in touch after the conference and talked regularly about business and life.

One day, we were catching up on the phone, and Kayla brought up that she was thinking of moving her business into another direction because she felt stagnate, and something else was calling her. I asked her what that something was, and she proceeded to tell me she had an influx of people recently reaching out to her to discuss her divorce and money story. Kayla was married at the age of nineteen but divorced at the age of twenty, with debt and no idea how she was going to pay the bills. This is a story that resonates with a lot of people but isn't told nearly as often as it should be. She said they were all so happy she was willing to share her story publicly about her divorce and how it affected her finances, as well as how she turned that around. I told her I regularly had people reaching out to me to discuss the very same thing, and I felt pulled to give people more resources. We decided we would join forces and create a platform to help others—not just women—figure out how to keep divorce from killing their finances. And Cash Wise Ex-Wives was born!

Now, in typical Type A, ass busting fashion, Kayla and I had this discussion, worked out an action plan to implement it, and implemented it all within a span of six weeks. This is on top of all of our other work and clients. No rest for the weary . . . or the crazy!

We had a brainstorming session to figure out what we were going to call ourselves, which is where Cash Wise Ex-Wives was born. During this search, we threw out a lot of names that had anything and everything to do with finances and divorce, but everything we came up with at first seemed to be already taken. Kayla kept finding availability for these other names with a .club extension, so it became a running joke that we were going to have to work .club into our platform at some point. I may still do that for a promotion, just as an inside joke to Kayla!

Once we figured out our name, we bought the URL that day and then started working on setting up the WP site. We both have access to a lot of free themes, so we decided the next meeting would be figuring out the theme and layout for the website. We did decide we didn't want it to be a blog because we simply don't have time for that. Our website https://cashwiseexwives.com is merely a platform to give people more information about us, what our business is about, and to get them signed up for the membership.

We decided the main platform would be a closed Facebook group where we would put a ton of useful content and have a weekly live chat.

Three of the monthly live chats are just Kayla and I discussing different topics within the divorce and finance space, but the fourth call is with a guest who has some level of expertise in a specific genre that ties into our platform. We always put a teaser out in our public FB group https://www.facebook.com/cashwiseexwives/ each week, just so people know what they're missing and can sign up to become members if they want to see the full content or be able to have access to the resources.

In order to get into this group, you have to become a member. But we made the plans super cheap because this is really a passion project for us both, and we just want to be able to get the resources out there for people to use. If we can help others avoid the same pitfalls we went through, then we have succeeded.

**56**

**What I Learned**

★ You never know where the next business opportunity is going to come from

★ Having a business partner who is very likeminded is extremely helpful with regards to productivity and staying on the same page

★ Having different strengths and weaknesses than your business partner makes a great working relationship and creates balance

★ Being able to help others is what I am really passionate about, whether we end up making a lot of money at it or not

# The Takeaway

After all of these different jobs, it would make sense that I had learned a thing or two. And if you look at the "What I learned" section under each job, I did learn at least one thing about myself and that business. But how does all of this help me today? Well, I suppose that is the real question.

If you couldn't tell, most of my jobs seemed to come to me via word of mouth. I'm a pretty friendly and chatty person by nature, so I guess that makes me memorable. But I also have a very unique skill set because of having all of these diverse jobs. I have learned to adapt to life so that it serves not only me but the people around me well. I constantly undersell myself, and that has got to be something unrelated to my noted diverse skills because I know I can do the job and do it well. This is something I am working on as I reflect back through all of the jobs I have run across in my life.

I still think diversity and learning to adapt are the keys to ultimate success and the freedom to do what you want to. For me, the things that make me happy are flexibility and freedom. I work harder than most people I know, and I am more than willing to do so, but I have to be given the right opportunity to thrive. That opportunity is to be left to my own devices with an end-goal in mind. As an entrepreneur, this is just how my brain is wired. I don't need a set of guidelines to follow because I have become very good at problem-solving.

In my opinion, to thrive in any work-life situation, you have to have the ability to do these few things:

- Adapt to any situation
- Know your skill set
- Have good problem-solving skills
- Use logic
- Have good time management skills
- Have integrity
- Have a strong work ethic
- Diversify and cross train
- Be willing to learn and grow
- Don't be afraid to walk away if you realize the job is no longer a good fit
- If you don't know the answer, ask questions!

If you can master those, it doesn't matter what your background is because you can succeed in any position that comes your way. So, here's to creating a better world for yourself and others by diversifying and adapting!

In health and love,
Shanah Bell

# Basic Guideline
# for Financial Stability

hen you decide to work more unconventionally, your finances are going to be considered unconventional, also. But this is not necessarily a bad thing. I have been doing this for quite a long time now and have found some pretty good tricks to help those of us who earn money through unconventional means to also create financial stability.

With that, here are a few of the things I would suggest to not only make your life easier but help you achieve financial stability, and possibly financial independence, while still living your unconventional life.

1. Keep a detailed budget and go through it weekly. Monthly is just not enough, when you have irregular income. I created a spreadsheet for this specific purpose back in 2002 and have been using it ever since. It has evolved in time, and is more in-depth now, but this is what has really helped me stay on track with my finances. The first month you do it, you won't really know what to budget in each category, realistically, so the best thing to do is to take an educated guess. Here is an example of the categories I use and how we structure the budget currently in our blended house of seven:

- Income–Varies, obviously

- Car/Auto–$1150.00

- Food/Beverages (Includes alcohol)–$800.00

- Recurring Bills–$1700.00

- Household–$300.00

- Clothing–$75.00

- Luxury–$200.00

- Gifts–$75.00

- Misc (Random one-off crap that doesn't fit in any other category)–$50.00

- TOTAL EXPENSES: $4,350.00

Anything we make over the $4350.00, or if we don't spend it all (which is *always* the goal), we put in savings or our Roth IRA's.

2. Open up a Roth IRA through a robo-advisor, such as Betterment, Ally Invest, SoFi, TD Ameritrade, Wealthfront, Wealthsimple, or any plethora of others that may be on the market now. The annual management rates vary by robo-advisor and sometimes by the amount of your portfolio, but the rates can start as low as .25% annually. We use Betterment, and ours falls into that .25% category. I really like Betterment because it was easy to set up, has one of the lowest annual management rates, and I can do everything from my phone, if I want to. This makes my life easier to see how my retirement fund is doing, or to transfer more money if it has been a good month. Depending on your situation, the best way I have found to put money into my

Roth IRA is to act like it is another bill. I also add it to my budget spreadsheet in the "bills" section so that it's accounted for in the budget every month. This makes it easier to stay on track for me. I set aside a certain amount a month that will be automatically withdrawn from my checking account and pretend it's a bill, not for funding my future self. But if your month is tight, and you don't feel that you can feasibly do that, then you don't have to set up automatic payments. I have just found that, when I say I'm going to fund the account and haven't set up automatic payments, it slips between the cracks. Even if you only have an extra $20 that month (but I am sure you can find more if you get creative), that is still better than nothing, especially if you are starting out when you're really young because you have the advantage of time and compounding interest. This is something I simply did not fully grasp when I was younger and I kick my younger self's ass everyday for her stupidity. Don't make my mistake! If you don't know what compounding is, then here is a great straight forward article that explains it: https://www.debtroundup.com/saving-investing-compound-interest-millions/

- Quick Example: Double $.01 every day for a month, and you end up with almost $11,000,000!

- Too bad the interest rate in the market isn't that great, but you get the drift.

3. After we put the allotted amount in our Roth IRA's, the rest gets moved into two different savings accounts. We are using MySavings-Direct.com right now because, at 2.40%, it has the highest interest rate in the market. This beats out our credit union by 220%! I don't

know about you, but I am perfectly fine with making 220% more interest on my money and it seems silly not to be. You can have as many as you like, but we currently have two.

- The first one is our Emergency Fund. This is the savings account you need for EMERGENCIES ONLY! An emergency is not drinks with a friend or a vacation—an emergency is something such as your car breaking down, a leak in your house, medical emergencies, not having work that month, or anything along those lines. Your Emergency Fund should have anywhere from three to six months of what you need to cover expenses in it.

**Example:**

As previously mentioned, our monthly budgeted expenses are $4,350.00. Multiply that by three, and you get $13,050.00, or by six, and you get $26,100.00. Obviously, it is better to have closer to six months worth of expenses in you emergency fund, but it will take a little while to build that up. The closer to six months you are, the more freedom you have with regards to choosing work that aligns better with what you are currently trying to do.

- The second savings account we have is for our travel fund. This is considered our "sacred cow," in that it's the thing we love to do the most but is not a necessity. We have a set amount we put into this account monthly, and we aren't allowed to travel if there is no money in there. So, when we have better months than others, we can throw more into it and treat ourselves to some traveling as a reward for our hard work and financial savviness. But if it's not a great month, then we can only put what we've got left over in there, which may not be much. Figure out what your one "sacred cow" is and create a separate savings account for that. When you see it grow to the point you can actually do what you want and not feel guilty or wonder how you are going to pay for it, THAT is freedom!

4. Another great trick to help build up your retirement savings is to use an app like Acorns. This app is tied to your credit card and/or checking account. It will round up to the nearest dollar of everything you spend and then invest that money into a retirement account you set up through the Acorns app. Not only that, but they have some newer features that include:

- If you shop with their sponsored vendors, then those merchants will also put money into your Acorns account with their "found money" feature.

- Using their "round-up multiplier" lets you set the amount invested to either two, three, or ten times the amount originally rounded up.

- Using their new "spend" account lets you set up a checking account with them to make your purchases with real time round-up options, as well as lets you invest up to 10% of your purchases from vendors not enrolled in their "found money" program.

Another alternative to Acorns is Stash, which does a lot of the same things, and sometimes they have promotions to in the beginning where they give you money right out of the gate to invest. There may be more of these sorts of apps floating around, so do your research and find the best fit for you. Either way, since these apps do the work for you, it not only makes your life easier because you don't have to think about it but it helps you get to the point of financial stability faster.

5. Last, but certainly not least, is to add in apps and browser extensions to increase your savings and sometimes even get free things. All of these are free, also, so don't be afraid to try a few different ones until you find what works for you. I use a multitude of them—all for different things—and have received quite a few free items just by using these in addition to what I'm already doing. Here is the current list of what I use:

- **Ebates** (https://www.ebates.com/r/JOURNE804?eeid=29041&utm_source=extension&utm_medium=raf_link) - This is a browser extension that you add to Chrome. You can also put it on your phone as an app and purchase through it that way. When you make a purchase online, while going through this extension/app first, it will give you cash back into your Ebates account. Once you have $25, it will automatically send it to your PayPal account to do whatever you please with it. I love this one!

- **Honey** (joinhoney.com/ref/muluwg) – This one is similar to Ebates, as it is also a browser extension. But instead of giving you cash back, it searches the internet for coupon codes for whichever site you happen to be on. Then, at checkout, it will tell you it found a certain number of coupons and ask if you want it to try them. Say yes, and it will run them all and then find the best deal. It's pretty awesome!

- **Ibotta** (https://ibotta.com/r/wnsxkvo) - This app is for your phone. It has a lot of stores tied to it such as Target and Home Depot. Choose which store you're going to, or already went to, and it will pull up a list of all of the current deals. Each item is worth a certain amount of money into your Ibotta account. Once you finish your shopping at each store, then redeem the items you purchased and scan your receipt with the app. On some items, you have to scan the barcode with the app when it asks you to, in order to prove you actually purchased the items. Once you do, and everything is accepted, the money goes into your Ibotta account. Once you hit $25, you can withdraw it at any time. You can either transfer the money into your PayPal account or put it on an Amazon gift card. I usually do the latter so I can have a credit to purchase pool chemicals from Amazon. I have been using this one for years, and it is great.

- **Receipt Hog** (https://app.receipthog.com/) – This is another app for your phone. I have been told it's difficult to get into this one because they are still smaller, and I got in as part of the beta group. But when you can get it (and hopefully that is now), this one is freaking fantastic! Every time I get a receipt, I take a picture of it with my app. It assigns a certain amount of coins to the purchase, depending on the store and the amount. Plus, there are bonus jackpot spins every week to get more coins—sort of like a slot machine, which is pretty fun to play. You can cash money out through PayPal or Amazon once you hit 2,500 coins. But I always wait until I get 6,500 coins because that gives me a $40 Amazon gift card. By combining this, and some Ibotta rewards, we got a free vacuum cleaner last year. Bonus!

- **GetUpside** (https://www.getupside.com/) – This is my newest love in the app world. They aren't everywhere yet, though, unfortunately. In my area, they are only good for gas stations and not groceries, which is still fine with me because I get plenty of gas driving all over hell's creation, taking kids places. This operates similarly to Receipt Hog, in that I have to take a picture of the receipt with the app. But before I get gas, I search on their map to see which stations offer the reward and how much it is for. Most times, I end up getting $.06 - $.15 off each gallon of gas I purchase. The payout system is the same as the others, in that once I hit $25 in my GetUpside account, I can cash out for money in my PayPal or on an Amazon gift card. These are pretty great additions to my regular savings plan!

When you get to the point where you have financial stability—even while working and living an unconventional life—you have reached the point of ultimate freedom. Now, you have the freedom to choose exactly what you want to do for work, and which skills you want to expand upon, without the stress and worry of making ends meet.

# About the Author

Shanah grew up in an entrepreneurial family, which drives her to think outside the box. As someone who hasn't stopped moving since her feet first hit the ground, she's not about to stop now. She is constantly on the hunt to learn new things and figure out how to attribute this new knowledge into her daily life.

She has a Master's of Nutrition degree, which she uses to help people learn how to heal themselves through dietary adaptation. She and her spouse have five children in a blended family, which can get a little bit crazy at times. But they love it and do everything they can to teach their children how to think outside the box, as well.

Her goal in life is not only to live her best life but to help everyone around her live theirs, also.

CPSIA information can be obtained
at www.ICGtesting.com
Printed in the USA
FFHW020800010319
50772573-56193FF